Josh Pila, whose astrological sign is Leo, drew this constellation to represent the lucky stars under which he was born. The lion is also a Jewish national and cultural symbol. To Josh, the lion signifies courage and strength. The addition of a soccer ball adds an element of fun and playfulness.

To family who perished ...
And the generations that never came to be

And to Josh and Bronia,
whose resilience and will to survive
ensured a brighter future.

UNDER A LUCKY STAR

MY FATHER'S STORY OF SURVIVAL AGAINST THE ODDS

RON PILA

First published in 2020
by Real Film and Publishing
www.realfp.com.au

Text © Ron Pila 2020
Images © The Pila Family 2020
Archival images © Holocaust Resarch Project

The moral rights of the author have been asserted.

All rights reserved. No part of this publication may be reproduced, stored in a retrieval system or transmitted in any form by any means, electronic, mechanical, photo-copying, recording or otherwise without the prior written permission of the author. Enquiries should be made to the publisher.

ISBN Paperback: 978-0-6488272-5-2

Edited by Georgie Raik-Allen
Editorial assistance by Romy Moshinsky
Designed by Patricia Garner
Typeset in Trajan and Sentinel
Printed & Bound by Ingram Spark

CONTENTS

FOREWORD—6

INTRODUCTION—8

INVASION—11

OCCUPATION—21

PUNKT—35

BUNKER—47

ESCAPE—55

ON THE OUTSIDE—71

ALONE—81

38 ADDRESSES—89

LIBERATION—101

RACHEL—109

REFUGEES & REUNIONS—117

OPERATION BRICHA—125

MUNICH—135

ALIYAH—144

IMMIGRANTS—151

ARMY—159

SAFE HARBOUR—168

MARY—173

THE LANCMANS—185

EPILOGUE—192

AFTERWORD—204

ACKNOWLEDGEMENTS—213

ABOUT THE AUTHOR—217

FOREWORD

**'In the beginning God created the heavens and the earth.
And the earth was without form, and void;
and darkness was upon the face of the deep.
And the Spirit of God moved upon the face of the waters.'**

GENESIS 1: 1, 2

The primordial sea features prominently in creation stories across the ancient world. We are fascinated by the sea, its beauty and its vastness. It is constantly in motion, both welcoming and forbidding, an immense, brooding giant.

Perhaps this fascination stems from the fact that the sea provides a perfect metaphor for the human story. Its shifting tides and currents, its impersonal latent power and its ebbs and flows. Like the past, the sea engenders both a sense of perspective and of awe.

Sometimes it seems that each of us is like a cork floating on the sea of history, buffeted by the tides and waves that wash over us: small, insignificant, powerless, at the mercy of greater forces. However, as we look more closely, we see that we are not merely passive spectators floating on the surface of history. Each of us is an integral part of the human story, in the same way that each individual drop of water is an essential component of the sea.

Our lives are experienced in the context of our times. To appreciate an individual, we must consider the times through which they lived. And to fully understand the past, we must view history from the perspective of the individuals who lived through it.

That is what I have endeavoured to do in this memoir of my father, Joshua (Josh) Pila. Josh has lived through, and has been an eyewitness to, some of the most significant events in 20th century history, certainly the modern Jewish story, including World War II and the Holocaust, post-war Europe, and the early years of the new State of Israel.

Much has already been written about these events; they are documented in countless books, movies and stories. I did not wish, nor am I qualified, to write a history book. Rather, I have endeavoured to peer beneath the surface and tell Josh's story, and, in doing so, bring to life a thin slither of the past.

INTRODUCTION

Josh Pila was born under a lucky star.[1]

He came into the world with his umbilical cord wrapped tightly around his neck. This can be dangerous at the best of times. In 1930s Poland, in a small town where children were born at home rather than in hospital and where the only medical assistance came from the local midwife, the dangers were multiplied.

Slavic tradition holds that being born with an umbilical cord around one's neck is a sign of good luck, but this was not the only sign that designated Josh as lucky. As a small baby, Josh became gravely ill with a roaring fever. Primitive medical treatments were unable to cure him and no-one expected him to survive. In desperation, his parents resorted to superstition, pouring melted candle wax over a broom to ward off evil spirits. Miraculously, Josh returned to good health.

Around the time that Josh recovered from this near fatal illness, both the local and global economies began to recover from the Great Depression. The highly industrialised region of Silesia, where

---

[1] Josh was named Szaja at birth. He adopted the name Joshua (in Hebrew, Yehoshua) shortly after arriving in Israel in 1949, effectively naming himself after one of the top soccer players in the Israeli soccer league. He is called Josh throughout this book, as that is how he is now known to his family and friends.

the Pila family lived, had suffered greatly in the economic downturn of the early 1930s. From the mid-1930s, when Josh was born, life improved significantly.

It seems ironic to describe a Jewish boy born in 1934 in southwestern Poland, close to the German border, as lucky. Statistically, his chances of survival were incredibly slim. Only about 10 percent of Polish Jews survived the Holocaust, most of them not on Polish soil. For Jewish children who remained in Poland during the war, the survival rate was a tiny fraction of one percent. During his most perilous moments, Josh's chances of survival dropped far lower still. His many cousins who lived in Poland when the war broke out perished. And yet, Josh was, and has always considered himself to be, lucky.

Josh's story is not just about luck. This is a story of resilience and courage, life-or-death decisions, fear, loss, sadness and inextinguishable hope.

Best of all, it is a survival story with a happy ending.

*JOSH'S HOMETOWN OF SOSNOWIEC
ON THE EVE OF WORLD WAR II*

INVASION

According to the history books, World War II began on a Friday, when the raging river of Nazism burst its banks and flooded neighbouring Poland. For Josh, the war began three days later, on a Monday.

* * *

On Friday 1 September 1939, without any declaration of war, Germany launched a massive ground and aerial attack along Poland's borders. Thus began World War II, the deadliest conflict in human history. Countries around the globe, including all major powers, were drawn into the hostilities. With few exceptions, European nations engaged in total warfare, requiring all of their military, economic and scientific resources, and leading to massive military and civilian casualties on all sides. Europe was ablaze, with no family or community left untouched.

The invasion of Poland came as no surprise, despite the non-aggression pact the two nations had signed in 1934. Hitler had flagged his aspirations for Germany to expand east to create 'living space' for ethnically German people in his book Mein Kampf, *published in 1925. Poland had been preparing to defend itself against Germany for some time. It prepared its lines of defence and entered into treaties with Great Britain and France.*

On 31 August 1939, the Germans staged a mock attack on a radio station in Gleiwitz as a 'false flag' to justify its attack on Poland. The protection of allegedly persecuted ethnic Germans living in Poland was also used as a pretext for war.

Despite the forewarning of Hitler's intentions, the Poles were ill-prepared and out-gunned. Poland's antiquated weapons were no match for Germany's modern military machine and 'blitzkrieg' tactics.[2] The Germans had newer planes, superior tanks and many more soldiers. Its army traversed Polish territory like a juggernaut, merciless and unstoppable, crushing all resistance in its path.

Poland's only hope was to hold out until its allies in the west initiated an offensive on Germany. However, Great Britain and France did not attack Germany and provided only limited military support. Instead, on 17 September 1939, Russia invaded a stricken and vulnerable Poland from the east. Only four weeks after the German invasion, Warsaw capitulated and Polish independence was lost, not to be restored for another five decades.

On Saturday 2 September 1939, Germany annexed the 'free city' of Danzig and Great Britain issued an ultimatum to Germany to withdraw from Poland.

On Sunday 3 September 1939, Great Britain, France, Australia and New Zealand formally declared war on Germany.

* * *

On Monday 4 September 1939, the German army marched into Sosnowiec[3], Josh's home town.

Mid-morning the following day, five-year-old Josh and his eight-year-old brother, Menasche[4], looked out from the window of their house as two German soldiers entered the courtyard of their building. The soldiers were young and of medium height and build.

---

2 The military tactic employed by the German army involving surprise, speed and superior firepower. 3 A town in the south-west of Poland. 4 His Polish name was Moniek.

They wore the distinctive steel helmets of the German army and the standard grey-green uniforms of the Wehrmacht.[5] Each held a rifle horizontally in one hand with the shoulder strap hanging almost to the ground.

Josh and Menasche, their noses pressed against the window, watched in stunned silence as the soldiers looked around for a few minutes and then left. They did not enter any of the buildings and it was far from clear what they were looking for.

Josh looked on with a mix of nervousness and curiosity. He knew that his parents and everyone in the town were strained with anxiety about the German invasion. The streets were empty as no-one ventured out to work or school that day; they stayed home and out of sight. Josh's mother, Bronia, busied herself in the kitchen, the tension accentuated by her tight-lipped silence.

The atmosphere was laden with a sense of foreboding. But those two soldiers did not do anything to justify that fear. Instead of being the monsters that Josh was expecting, the Nazis appeared to be ordinary men.

This benign first impression of the German occupation gave Josh no indication of the horrors to come.

* * *

Sosnowiec is a relatively young city by European standards; earliest references to the city date back only as far as the early 18th century. It is located in the Zaglebie region of south-west Poland, close to the then German border. The name 'Sosnowiec' means 'pinewood' and is a reference to the pine trees that once grew in the region.

Sosnowiec developed into a mining and industrial town in the 19th century after the discovery of large deposits of black coal in the

---

[5] The unified armed forces of Nazi Germany.

area. It was built on a grid, rather than around a market square as was the norm for medieval towns. The development of Sosnowiec was a product of modernity, its rapid growth was driven by one of the great technological innovations of the time: steam-driven railway engines.

The nearby medieval towns lay on the merchant routes between major commercial centres, such as Krakow and Warsaw. Though often small, these towns were important outposts for travellers seeking safe shelter overnight, and much of their economies were built around providing hospitality services (rooms, meals, and entertainment) to travelling merchants.

The economies of towns on the merchant routes changed dramatically in the late 19th century with the implementation of railway systems. Railways provided quicker and safer transportation than the traditional horse and cart, allowing for the distances between major commercial centres to easily be traversed within a day and making redundant the hospitality services provided in the small towns along the way. Many inhabitants of those towns had no choice but to move to the more recently established industrial cities in search of employment.

Jews started arriving in Sosnowiec around this time. They moved from small ancient towns, where life had remained relatively unchanged for hundreds of years, to a modern city with electricity, household plumbing and a comprehensive tram system. At the same time, large numbers of Poles, including Polish Jews, moved across the seas to America, the 'land of opportunity'. This was not possible for all, and so the Jews who moved to Sosnowiec referred to the city as 'little America'.

Steadily, the community increased in size and the Great Synagogue was built at 16 Dekerta Street just before the turn of the 20th century. Over the following years, the Jewish community grew, *and by 1939, Jews numbered around 25,000 of a total population of 100,000.*

Sosnowiec had a rich and thriving Jewish community, with every Jewish religious and political movement represented including Chasidim, Bundism, Mizrachism and Zionism. In 1927, Ze'ev Jabotinsky, leader of the Revisionist Zionist movement, came to visit. His charismatic speeches attracted followers and a Revisionist[6] chapter in Sosnowiec was established.

The Jewish community of Sosnowiec was typical of Jewish communities throughout Poland. While the Jews lived among and alongside their non-Jewish neighbours, they were not fully integrated or assimilated. They spoke a mix of Yiddish and Polish and led traditional religious Jewish lifestyles, keeping kosher and honouring the Sabbath. Jews and non-Jews did interact but, in the main, Jews largely kept to themselves, buying goods in Jewish shops and attending Jewish schools.

Jews also tended to gravitate to certain neighbourhoods, often centred around synagogues. The residents of Dekerta Street, home to the Great Synagogue and the Jewish market, and the surrounding streets, were almost all Jewish.[7]

* * *

The families of Josh's parents had been part of the migration of Jews into Sosnowiec from regional towns. Josh's father, Solomon[8], was born in 1904 in Wodzislaw, a small town west of Krakow. The family moved to Wolbrom and then on to Sosnowiec shortly thereafter.

The Pilas had been butchers and livestock traders. As the eldest son, it was natural for Solomon to follow his father into the family business. He was smart and ambitious despite his limited schooling, and was keen to take the business further. He carved out

---

[6] The Revisionists advocated a more assertive and militant approach to achieving their Zionist goals–to establish a Jewish homeland–than other Zionist factions. [7] The few non-Jews who lived in the neighbourhood were employed to caretake the buildings and act as '*Shabbos goys*'. Jews strictly honouring the Sabbath would not flick a light switch, turn on a heater or light an oven during the Sabbath. To get around these restrictions, they would pay a non-Jew to do it for them. [8] In Polish, Szlama.

a niche as a manufacturer and seller of smallgoods, one of the few Jewish butchers in the area to do so. He ran a small manufacturing facility and shop in the food market at 7 Dekerta Street, diagonally across the road from the Great Synagogue.

Solomon was serious and considered by the broader family to be highly intelligent. He was a deep thinker, interested in issues broader than his daily existence. He read widely about politics and world events and was aware of the precarious position that Jews occupied in the Polish community. Like many in the Jewish community, he believed Zionism offered the best solution to the Jewish predicament. He longed for the creation of a Jewish homeland and would have moved his immediate family to Palestine if not held back by his commitment to the Pila family business.

Solomon was captivated by the words of Ze'ev Jabotinsky when he visited Sosnowiec in 1927 and became a senior member of the local Revisionist movement. He sat on the committee that assessed funding proposals for young Revisionists wanting to make *aliyah* (immigrate to Palestine). Solomon was highly respected and well connected in the community.

Josh's mother, Bronia (nee Lancman), was born in Sosnowiec in 1906, but her family had, in the late-19th century, moved from Wislica, a small town with an important medieval heritage, which had been in decline for some time. The Lancmans had lived in Wislica since at least the mid-18th century and had developed a reputation as high quality tailors.

In Sosnowiec, Bronia's very religious family lived in a ground floor apartment at 14 Dekerta Street, immediately next door to the Great Synagogue. As well as being fine tailors, many of the Lancman family had beautiful singing voices and were members of the Jewish choir, even performing with the world-renowned tenor Jan

Kiepura, one of Sosnowiec's most famous sons. On Friday nights, when the Lancman family gathered around the dining table and sang Shabbat songs, the other residents of 14 Dekerta Street filled the courtyard to listen to the beautiful harmonies.

Bronia's mother died of tuberculosis when Bronia was 12 years old, and, as the oldest girl in a family of seven children, Bronia took over many of the maternal responsibilities in the household. As a young woman, she also had a job in a clothes shop on Modrzejowska Street, the main commercial street in Sosnowiec. After she married, she worked in Solomon's smallgoods business. Bronia was diligent and a hard worker, strong willed and determined—attributes that she drew on as the war progressed.

As a young boy, Josh spent a great deal of time at the smallgoods shop. He would stand on a ledge so that he could peer over the counter and watch his parents interact with customers. This proved to be highly educational, providing Josh important lessons about money and commercial transactions. He was attentive to detail, inquisitive and a quick learner. At the age of four, he remarked to his mother that they could make more profit if they increased their prices.

Josh was a small boy with a slight build and fair skin while his older brother Menasche was taller, darker, with a bigger build. The two were also very different in personality. Josh was disobedient, determined and cheeky. Younger than most of his cousins, he was often left out of their games. This he refused to accept, insinuating himself and ruining their fun. He was the subject of a steady stream of complaints to his aunts and uncles. Menasche was the quieter, more patient and more conservative of the brothers. His was a gentle soul and he never beat up his smaller brother for ruining their games.

Both Solomon and Bronia came from large families, so there were always lots of aunts, uncles and cousins nearby. Most of their socialising was with the extended family.

The Pila family lived at 1 Sienkewicza Street. Three buildings stood within the gated compound, including a two-storey building at the back of the block that comprised four apartments. Josh's family lived in the ground floor apartment on the left. The other ground floor apartment was occupied by Solomon's sister, Esther, her husband and two daughters, the Lichtig family. The two upstairs apartments were occupied by other, unrelated families. Solomon's parents lived in the second building in the compound, together with Solomon's youngest brother, Karl.

The third building, at the front of the compound, housed the property caretaker, an older man whose responsibilities included tending the vegetable gardens, stacking coal, potatoes and cabbages in the cellars, and acting as the *Shabbos goy*.[9]

***

In October 1939, Germany formally annexed Upper Silesia (including Sosnowiec), West Prussia and Poznan into the Third Reich. These areas had been part of Germany before World War I, with the exception of Sosnowiec, which had previously been part of Russia. The rest of German-occupied Poland was administered by a German appointed governor general, Nazi party member, Hans Frank, and was called the General Government.

***

Although it was still the tail end of summer, a darkness descended on Sosnowiec, like the ominous and threatening clouds that herald a major storm. It was a far cry from the carefree summer Josh's

---

9 See footnote 7

family had just spent in the hills of Zakopane in southern Poland, near the Czechoslovakian border. That August, they had hired a house for three weeks with Josh's cousins, aunt and uncle. Josh had enjoyed the scenery from the train ride through the picturesque mountains and the fun had rolling down the lush green hills with his cousins.

* * *

The Jewish community received the news of the German invasion with great trepidation. They had heard stories about the Nazi regime's policies toward Jews and the many ways Jews were being persecuted in areas controlled by the Germans.

At a time when communications were limited and the only social media was word-of-mouth rumours, Jewish families anxiously weighed up their best alternatives for survival. "Fighting-aged men will be killed or conscripted into slave labour." "The German army will take all of our food—we will starve." "We are better off in the country with the farmers... in the city... in Russia..."

Locals packed their most precious belongings and rushed to railway stations to escape to the east. Carriages were packed to breaking point when the trains pulled out, but many were stranded just a short time after departure when bombed rail lines prevented Jews and other panicked residents from fleeing.

Hundreds of thousands of Jews, travelling by horse and cart, car, or on foot, fled from the advancing Germans into eastern Poland. From there, many thousands crossed the borders—north into Lithuania or south into Hungary or Romania.

Later, when the Russians occupied eastern Poland, they deported large numbers of Jews, along with thousands of non-Jewish Poles, whom they identified as 'unreliable elements', to Siberia, central Asia and other remote Soviet destinations. While these refugees suffered great hardships and many died from starvation and disease, they were out of reach of the Nazi armies and spared the industrialised killing that defined the Holocaust.

* * *

Those with access to a horse and cart were better placed to make the dash east. Included in this exodus were Solomon and four of his brothers Usher, Victor, Zalman and Joseph. As butchers and manufacturers of smoked sausages they had a horse and cart used for the delivery of products to customers. The Pila brothers left on 2 September 1939, Saturday evening, after the end of the Sabbath. They made the heart-wrenching decision to leave their families on the assumption that only the men were at risk and that the women and children left behind would be safe. They were not alone in this thinking. Many Jewish men left during the first days of the war.

They returned to Sosnowiec 10 days later, having realised how dangerous the Nazi occupation was for all Jews, regardless of gender or age. Solomon and his brothers could not bear to be away from their families when all Jews were exposed to life-threatening risks. Josh and his family were very relieved to have Solomon back.

GREAT SYNAGOGUE IN SOSNOWIEC ON DEKERTA STREET, NEXT DOOR TO BRONIA'S FAMILY'S APARTMENT BLOCK

OCCUPATION

The treatment of the residents of German-occupied Poland was brutal. As a matter of course, the Nazis used terror and collective punishment to control civilian populations and break down resistance. Mass shootings, beatings and theft of property were common. Although clearly contrary to international laws, there was no recourse or appeals process available against these abuses. While both Poles and Jews were victims of these tactics, Jews were targeted more viciously.

* * *

The impact of the occupation on the Jews of Sosnowiec was immediate. From the very first day they were subjected to random shootings, destruction of property and the roundup of able-bodied men to be sent to work camps.

The Great Synagogue on Dekerta Street, just a few hundred metres from the Pila's home, was burned down on 9 September 1939. The loss of the synagogue, so central to the community's day-to-day life, was devastating. Josh's parents tried to shield him and his brother, but Josh was aware of the outrage and despair emanating from those around him. He saw adults openly sobbing in the streets, crying for the loss of their beloved synagogue, and in fear of the hardships to come.

GERMAN POLICE IN SOSNOWIEC

Almost immediately, Jews were subject to significant restrictions on economic activity, interactions with non-Jews, and where they could live or even walk. Many Jewish businesses were shut down. Jews were not allowed to shop in non-Jewish shops or to serve non-Jews in Jewish shops. They were forbidden from travelling on trams, buses or trains. These restrictions were the early steps in an ongoing process intended to isolate the Jews, with the ultimate aim of removing them from society altogether.

The penalties for breaking these rules were extremely harsh and Josh's parents made sure he knew exactly which places and streets he must avoid.

Fortunately, Solomon's business as a butcher and manufacturer of deli goods was considered 'essential' and allowed to continue. The fact that sausages and smoked meats were so popular with the German occupiers and the local Poles proved to be a big advantage for Josh's family in their struggle to survive the ordeals ahead.

When Jewish children were forbidden from going to school, Josh's parents hired a private tutor to teach Menasche at home. Although Josh was not allowed to interrupt these lessons, he was able to look over his brother's shoulder, as he was taught to read and write and do basic arithmetic. This indirect tuition was Josh's only form of education for many years, although by the end of the war, Josh could read and write in Polish and German.

The streets became increasingly dangerous. Jews of working age were rounded up and sent to work camps for forced labour in industries that assisted the Nazi war effort. Sometimes the Judenrat, the Jewish council, would be asked to identify a certain number of people for this purpose. Other times Jews would be taken from the streets and sent away with no warning. They simply did not return home, to the distress of their families who then had to fend for themselves. Sometime in 1941, two of Josh's uncles, Zalman and Joseph Pila, were rounded up in this way and sent to a work camp. Although they were able to send and receive letters and parcels until mid-1942, the family never saw them again.

From early in the occupation, Jews were required to wear an arm band to signify that they were Jewish. The arm bands were white with a blue *Magen David* (Star of David), and were handed out by the Judenrat when people registered for food coupons. In May 1941, the arm bands were replaced by a yellow *Magen David*, with the word 'Jude' written in the middle of the star, which had to be worn on the left breast of every shirt, jacket and coat.

In order to further control the Jewish community, the Germans imposed heavy penalties for even minor infringements. Walking on the wrong street could lead to arrest and execution, either by shooting or hanging. Public hangings were conducted regularly in the garden in the centre of town.

The Jews were forced to witness the hangings and the bodies would be left dangling for several days as a deterrent to others. Three to six people would be hung at a time. The scaffolding would be wheeled in by horse and the ropes tied to sturdy branches in the trees. The condemned person would stand on the scaffolding with their hands tied behind them and the rope around their necks. When the horses pulled the scaffolding away, they would dangle above the ground, their bodies twitching and struggling for a few minutes before they became still, their swollen tongues hanging out of their mouths. Family members would wail and cry while the rest of the crowd stood silently, shocked and frightened.

Josh witnessed several public hangings. He looked on with deep revulsion, anger and disbelief that people could treat their fellow humans with such brutality.

In 1940, when Jews were prohibited from travelling to other towns without permission, two of Josh's uncles, Usher and Victor Pila, travelled illegally to Wolbrom to purchase a cow for their butcher shop. They were arrested and locked up at the police station less than 100 metres from Josh's house.

Solomon's family asked Bronia to go to the police station to advocate for Usher and Victor because she spoke German well. The building occupied by the police station also housed the German headquarters for the Zaglebie region and was strictly out of bounds for Jews. For Bronia to go to the police station was fraught with danger; she could have been arrested or shot for merely walking in that area.

Bronia relented to the family's pressure, and with great trepidation, went to the police station and asked to see the chief, who was known to be a particularly cruel and sadistic man. Bronia was, however, granted an audience with another senior official and she told him a story that the brothers had not known it was illegal to leave town, were under pressure to provide food for their children, and so on. The fact that the cow was to be used to make the sausages and deli items that the Germans were so fond of may also have helped. The official was sympathetic and released the two brothers, saving them from almost certain death. Both ultimately survived the war.

Bringing arrested Jews home in this way was virtually unprecedented and word spread around the community quickly. Family members of others in similar predicaments approached Bronia and begged her to intervene on the part of loved ones who had been arrested. Reluctantly, she had to decline because the dangers were too great. After the release of the brothers, Bronia went once more to the police station to deliver a package of smallgoods to the official as a thank you. She didn't make this gesture until they were released as she did not want to be accused of attempting to bribe him.

The rapport Bronia built with the German official proved to be very helpful to the family. The official came to lunch at Josh's house while they were still living on Sienkewicza Street. He was in his early forties, tall, impressive and very German looking, with piercing blue eyes. He wore a uniform and carried the rank of captain, although this didn't necessarily mean that he actively served in the army. It was standard practice for German civil administrators during the war to wear army uniforms and carry army ranks. The official was friendly as he was introduced to the family. He was particularly partial to steak tartare.

The German official visited the family again much later on, when they were living in the Srodula ghetto. On that occasion, Josh didn't see him because he was secreted away in a hiding place.

* * *

Jewish communities have always been very good at organising themselves. Wherever they are, they quickly form committees to provide welfare for those in need and to advocate with non-Jewish authorities.

A new Jewish committee (Judenrat) was formed in Sosnowiec on 6 September 1939, in the very first days of the occupation, by order of the Germans. Members of the pre-war Jewish committees generally did not want to cooperate with, or facilitate the endeavours of the Nazis. Accordingly, new members were appointed, mainly opportunists motivated primarily by furthering their own interests or prospects of survival.

The Judenrat did provide some valuable services such as welfare and support to families when the husband and father was taken, for example, to a labour camp. However, the organisational layer established by the Judenrat also assisted the Germans to systematically persecute the Jews. The Judenrat held the names and addresses of all the Jewish families in a particular area. When the Germans wanted to deport a set number of Jews, they merely detailed their requirements to the Judenrat which would then identify, select and even round up people. The moral dilemmas faced by Judenrat members throughout the occupied territories were complex and intractable. To many in the community, they were collaborating with the Germans.

Reporting to the Judenrat was a Jewish police force. The role of the police force was to make sure that Jews abided by the rules, which often included tracking down those Jews that sought to defy German orders. In particular, the Jewish militia assisted the authorities in hunting down the small Jewish resistance groups that were active in the area.

There were only very minor incidences of armed resistance by Jews in Sosnowiec. Resistance groups did not have the weapons, resources or numbers to wage direct confrontations. However, they were able to resist in more indirect ways: stealing German army correspondence and passing it on to the Polish underground; sending letters to German businessmen describing the atrocities committed by the Nazis in Poland and imploring them to rise up against the regime; and displaying posters urging Jews to disobey German orders. The Germans retaliated, threatening retribution against family members of the Judenrat and the Jewish militia if they did not act to quash this resistance.

The Jewish community became increasingly distrustful of the Judenrat. Many believed the committee, and in particular its leadership, were primarily concerned with saving their own lives and gaining preferential treatment. A great deal of resentment built up against the Judenrat and the Jewish militia. Ultimately, those individuals did not fare better than the rest of the community. Despite the promises made by the German occupiers, the Judenrat and Jewish militia had witnessed too many Nazi crimes to be allowed to survive.

* * *

In the early days of the occupation, Josh and his cousins liked to play war games. They would pretend to be German or Polish soldiers and stage make-believe battles. A stick, with a piece of string as a shoulder strap, would serve as a rifle. Ironically, in these games, Josh would prefer to be a German soldier, as he liked to be on the 'winning' team.

Josh and Menasche were instructed by their parents to stay at home, safe from the terrible dangers lurking on the streets. But their parents worked long hours every day and were not able to supervise the brothers. Consequently, the boys spent large parts of the day on the streets, forming gangs and fighting. Almost every day, gangs of Jewish kids and gangs of non-Jewish kids would throw stones and rocks at each other. As he was still very small, and much to his disappointment, Josh's role was limited to stone 'collector'. He would gather stones as ammunition for the bigger boys. Menasche, on the other hand, was a stone 'thrower'.

During this time, war-time rations for food and other essentials were implemented throughout most of the world. For civilians in occupied territories the restrictions were particularly harsh and for the Jewish populations in those territories they were even more severe. Generally, the number of calories allocated to each Jewish person was below the minimum daily requirement for subsistence. Hunger and the struggle to obtain enough food to survive were a pervasive part of every day.

Food was rationed through monthly coupons. Each person—adult or child—was issued a monthly coupon card about the size of an A5 sheet of paper with the individual's name in the centre. Around the outside of the card were small tickets for individual food items—bread, margarine, meat, sugar—that could be exchanged at the relevant shop. The shopkeeper would cut out the ticket and stick it into the shop's ledger to account for the goods sold. Some items were interchangeable; a coupon for sugar could be used for jam, for example.

A range of coupons, each with their own colour representing a different mix of entitlements, were allocated to people depending on the nature of their job. Those employed in manual labour considered important for the Nazi war effort had a greater food allowance so that they could remain fit and strong. Young children and adults with less important jobs were given more meagre food rations. Jews were allotted the lowest rations of all. Life was not sustainable on these rations and Jews were slowly starving to death.

Josh's family felt the impact of these restrictions, as did all members of the community. Family meals were smaller and 'delicacies' like butter and coffee were simply not available. Tea was brewed from dried apple peel. Food that could be purchased without coupons, such as potatoes and cabbage, were in great demand and made up the bulk of their diet along with staples such as oats and semolina.

Even with coupons, obtaining food was a challenge. People lined up for hours, often to be turned away empty-handed when the shop's supplies ran out. Children were especially useful for waiting in lines while their parents worked.

(LEFT) PUBLIC HANGING IN SOSNOWIEC. JOSH WITNESSED SEVERAL OF THESE EVENTS (RIGHT) MAP OF SOSNOWIEC DURING THE OCCUPATION, DRAWN BY JOSH PILA

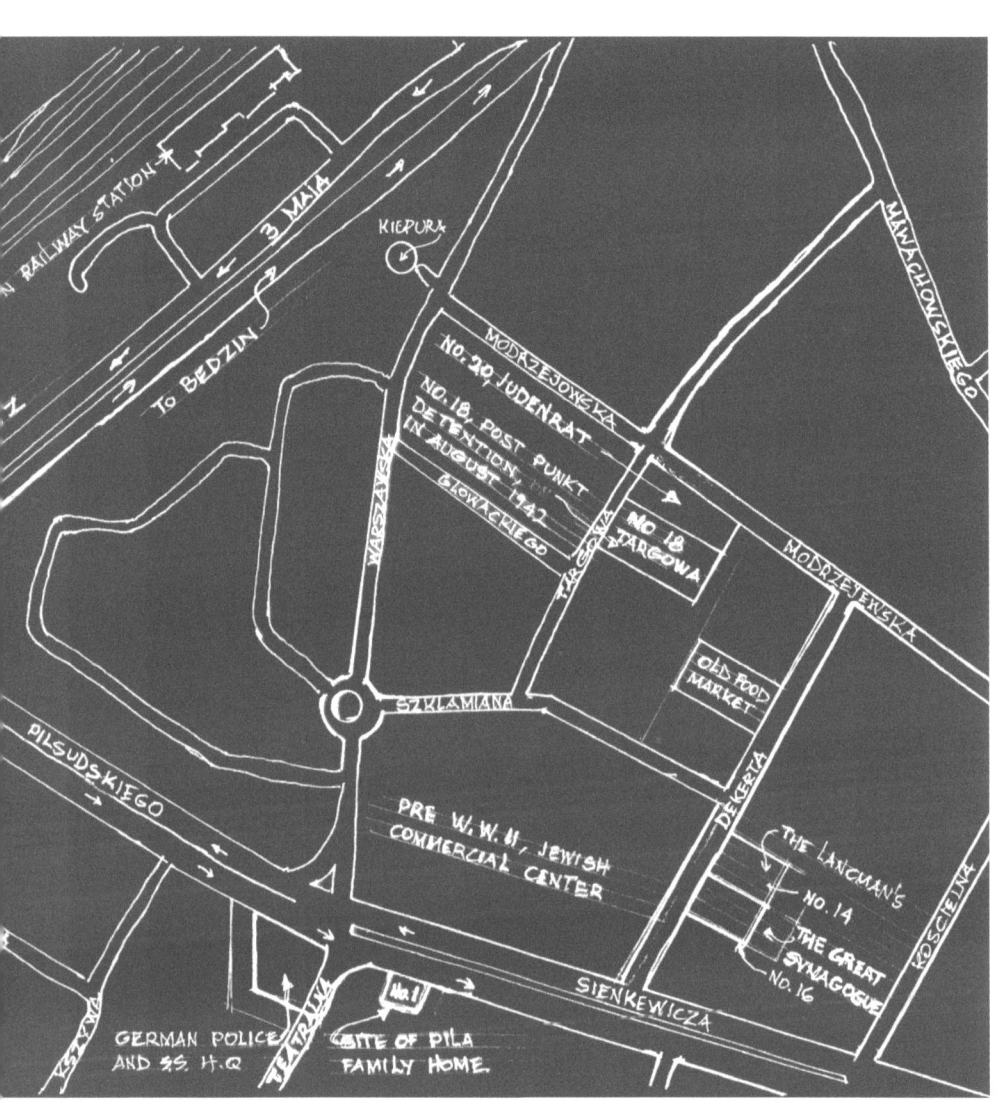

As is inevitable in times of war, a thriving black market developed. Trading on the black market was illegal, and there were severe, often fatal, consequences for those who were caught. Still, for those faced with starvation, it was a risk worth taking.

Despite these restrictions, Josh did not suffer greatly from hunger. He trained himself to only feel hungry when he could smell food that he knew was his to eat. The fact that his family was in the food business was a big advantage. They had ready access to meat for themselves and could swap meat products on the black market for other foodstuffs. Throughout the war, lack of food did not cause Josh to suffer too much.

* * *

Amid the hardships and struggles, life went on. Although unplanned, Bronia fell pregnant and gave birth to a beautiful baby girl, Rachel,[9] in September 1941. As was customary in those days, the birth took place at home, in the main bedroom of the apartment in Sienkewicza Street. Bronia was assisted by her sister Fela, who was staying with the family, and a midwife.

Josh and Menasche were not allowed into the bedroom during the birth, but came in soon after to cuddle their new sister. This was a new experience for Josh, holding a tiny baby for the first time. He was transformed to the role of older brother and instinctively felt the need to protect his little sister. Josh, like all of his family, had mixed feelings about this arrival: their natural excitement tempered by unease about bringing a baby into such a hostile world.

The birth of Rachel provided a rare occasion for celebration, even if somewhat muted. The apartment filled with family members to drink a celebratory toast of kiddush wine (*l'chaim*) and eat the traditional sponge cake (*lekach*) which Fela had quickly baked.

---

10 In Polish, Ruchla or Rachela.

The towns in the Silesian and Zaglebie regions that had been annexed into the Third Reich comprised, as well as Jews, a mix of ethnically German and Polish (or Slavic) populations. The Nazi intention was to clear the towns for 'living space' by removing all Poles and Jews— other than a small proportion of Poles to be used as slave labour.

Jews from Katowitz[11], and the surrounding towns including Bismarckhutte[12], Koenigshutte[13] and Gleiwitz[14], were expelled from their homes and forced east. The German civil authorities in that region would have liked to relocate them into the General Government but Hans Frank, the governor of the General Government, refused to take them. Instead, the relocated Jews were crammed into Sosnowiec and the nearby town of Bedzin.

At the same time, the Jews in Sosnowiec were forced to move into the older, poorer parts of the town. This area is often referred to as an 'open ghetto', as there were no fences or guards keeping them in. With the influx of Jews from other towns, the open ghetto became incredibly crowded. Housing had to be shared, with more than one family often forced to share a single room, and facilities and amenities stretched beyond capacity. People were starving, diseases were rampant, and morale was rapidly deteriorating.

* * *

In late 1941, Jews living on the main roads of Sosnowiec, including Sienkewicza Street, were moved to the open ghetto where the Judenrat allocated apartments for them. Josh's family were moved into a small two-bedroom apartment on the first floor of a four-storey building.

Around this time, the Germans also relocated all the Jews from the town of Oswiecim[15] into neighbouring towns such as Sosnowiec. An older couple was allocated to Josh's apartment in the open ghetto and occupied one of the two bedrooms. The man was overweight and

---

[11] During the occupation this town was known as Katowitz but is now known by its Polish name, Katowice. [12] During the occupation, this town was known as Bismarckhutte, but is now known by its Polish name, Chorzow Batory. [13] During the occupation this town was known as Koenigshutte, but is now known by its Polish name, Chorzow. [14] During the occupation this town was known as Gleiwitz, but is now known by its Polish name, Gliwice. [15] Oswiecim is the Polish name of a town in south-west Poland, about 30 kilometres from Sosnowiec, where the Auschwitz extermination camp was located.

unwell and his wife treated him every day with leeches, which she kept in a large jar.

For Josh, this intrusion was just another hardship imposed on the family in an ongoing cycle of persecution and oppression. The couple were taken away sometime later and Josh's family never saw them again.

* * *

For three years after the German occupation in 1939, within the constraints of terrible hardships, food shortages, disease, random abductions, violence, draconian rules and punishments, life (of a fashion) went on for Josh and the Jews of Sosnowiec.

Then, in August 1942, the oppression and persecution of the Jews entered a terrifying new phase.

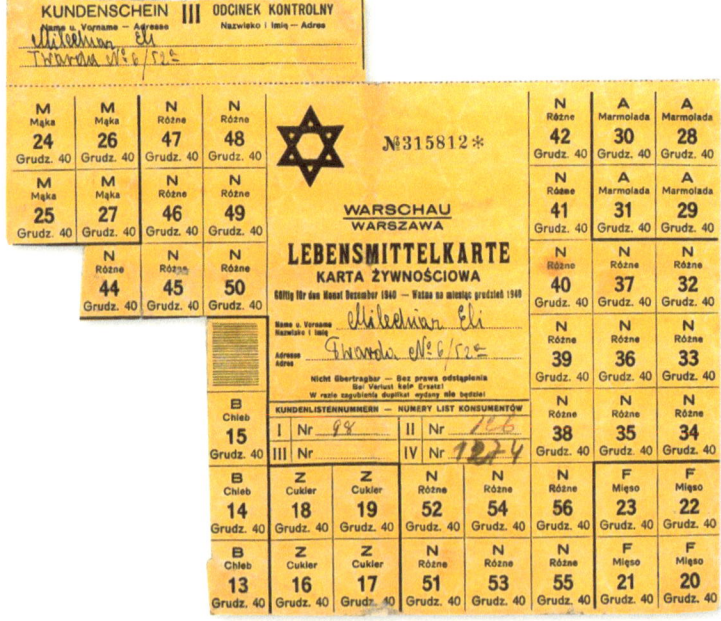

A SAMPLE FOOD COUPON CARD USED IN WARSAW

PUNKT

On Wednesday 12 August 1942, a beautiful summer's day in Sosnowiec, Josh Pila was sentenced to death.

* * *

The German word *'punkt'* means a point or dot. Sometimes, it is used to refer to a meeting place. It is also the term used by the Jews of Sosnowiec to refer to an event in August 1942, an event that served as a punctuation mark designating the end of the early occupation and the beginning of a new and far more sinister phase in their persecution. An event that began with the gathering of the Jews at a central meeting place.

* * *

Anti-Jewish sentiment had been prevalent throughout Europe for centuries. Religious factors underpinned traditional anti-Semitism. The deeply Catholic Polish public were for centuries told by their religious leaders that Jews had killed Jesus and that Jewish rituals required the murder of young Christians and the draining of their blood, the so-called 'blood libel'. Furthermore, Jews had often been engaged by Polish nobles and landlords to manage their estates. So, for many Polish peasants, Jews were the human representation of oppression and inequality. The fact that some Jews were also engaged in money lending added to the bitterness and resentment directed at them from the poorer classes.

The Nazis tapped into these embedded and enduring sentiments. Hitler had flagged his conviction that the Jews had to be removed from society long before he came to power. His book, Mein Kempf (My Struggle), *written while he was in prison in 1924 for his part in a failed plot to overthrow the Weimer government, was full of anti-Jewish rhetoric.*

Hitler blamed the Jews for starting World War I and for Germany's ultimate defeat in that war. He was convinced that Germany had been stabbed in the back by treacherous enemies within—namely communists and Jews. He also blamed Jews for the Great Depression, which caused significant misery to an already downtrodden German population. According to his lunatic views, Jews were responsible for the opposing evils of both capitalism and communism.

Hitler and the Nazis wanted to remove the Jews first from any position of influence and then from society altogether. They started to develop plans to deport all Jews out of the greater German territories. Initially they looked to Madagascar and subsequently they planned to export the Jews to Siberia once they had completed their conquest of the Soviet Union.

Sometime during 1941, the Nazis changed their approach. They decided it would be more efficient to exterminate the Jews in their entirety rather than relocate them. A large number of Nazi leaders across various government agencies began work on a plan to annihilate 11 million European Jews. They needed to accelerate the process so that they could exterminate large numbers as quickly as possible. This culminated on 20 January 1942 when 15 Nazi leaders met at a villa in the Berlin suburb of Wannsee to ratify plans for the so-called 'Final Solution'.

The Final Solution called for the industrial-scale killing of Jews in gas chambers at specially designed extermination camps. New camps were built and existing concentration camps were 'upgraded' to introduce this extermination capability. The largest and best known of these camps was in the Polish town of Oswiecim.

Oswiecim, in south-west Poland, has a thousand-year history, and for many centuries, held a large Jewish population. In 1940, the Germans established a concentration camp on the outskirts of the town primarily to incarcerate Polish dissidents. That camp was known by the German name for the town, Auschwitz. To make room for the camp, thousands of residents, including Jews, were evicted and relocated, many to Sosnowiec, barely 30 kilometres to the north-west.

In late 1941, construction of Auschwitz II-Birkenau commenced, initially to house prisoners of war before it was repurposed as a concentration and extermination camp designed for the efficient killing of Jews. Train tracks led to a railway platform in the middle of the camp, a short walk from the gas chambers. The first gas chamber began operating in March 1942. Other gas chambers and crematoria soon followed. When a transport of Jews arrived, while a few were selected to work in the camp, most were taken immediately to the gas chambers and killed.

Other extermination camps in Poland were built and came into operation during a similar time period, including Chelmno (December 1941), Belzec (March 1942), Majdanek (March 1942), Sobibor (May 1942) and Treblinka (July 1942).

With the extermination facilities up and running, the Nazis were ready to start collecting and transporting Jews to the death camps in large numbers.

* * *

While the Nazis had been killing and deporting the Jews of Sosnowiec since the occupation began, the Germans took a dramatic step in August 1942 to implement the Final Solution. Until that time, the Nazis had been deporting fit, working-age Jews to slave labour camps to help in the war effort, and the killing of Jews had been sporadic. Now, with the death camps at Auschwitz and elsewhere ready for operation, the Nazis moved to round up and deport those who were considered to be of no use to the regime—'useless mouths' as they were referred to.

The Germans announced that all the Jews of Sosnowiec must assemble at the town's main soccer field on 12 August 1942 to be registered and issued new food coupons. The Jews were wary of the Germans' intentions and worried that gathering in one place would expose them with nowhere to run or hide. To ensure high attendance, the Germans undertook a significant propaganda exercise to disguise their murderous intentions. Each Jewish family was officially and individually notified two weeks in advance. Leading up to the event, vans with loudspeakers drove through the streets making announcements. The Germans promised that all attendees would be sent home after the census with their papers stamped and new food coupons issued. Those not at the gathering would be denied the food entitlements that were essential to basic survival.

A similar event occurred in Bedzin, a town with a comparable Jewish population, just six kilometres away. To aid in the deception, three similar events were held in July 1942 in the nearby small towns of Czelodz, Strzemieszyc and Modrzejow, which only involved a relatively small number of Jews. In those towns, the Jews who attended were registered, provided with coupons and sent straight home. This ruse gave the Jews of Sosnowiec and Bedzin the intended false sense of security.

On the appointed day, as ordered, thousands of Jews, including Josh and his family, assembled on the soccer field. There were no German authorities or soldiers to be seen. Many people brought picnic rugs and food; the large crowd and sense of occasion provided for a carnival type atmosphere. It took many hours for all the Jews to congregate on the field. Friends and family socialised and chatted.

The sudden arrival of a menacing presence extinguished the festive atmosphere. Seemingly out of nowhere, truckloads of heavily armed German soldiers and members of the SS appeared and surrounded the stadium. Machine guns were trained on every exit route.

A hush fell over the crowd. Like swimmers playing in the ocean who suddenly realise they are surrounded by predatory sharks, every person in the stadium was consumed with dread. What does this mean? What is going to happen? Why have we come here?

Multiple tables were set up around the ground manned by SS officers. Terrified families were required to line up in alphabetical order and approach the tables where a German officer scrutinised each individual and assigned them to a category. The 'selection' process was arbitrary and completely at the discretion of the presiding officer. His fateful decisions could not be argued or appealed.

Jews were allocated into one of four categories:

CATEGORY ONE: Those already employed in factories or other works deemed essential to the German war effort. People in this category generally already had papers ('*sonders*') identifying the work that they were involved in. These papers were invaluable in avoiding deportation.

CATEGORY TWO: Those who would be forced into labour, again to further the war effort. They were set aside for deportation to labour camps.

CATEGORY THREE: Those whose worth to the Germans was undecided.

These people were ultimately released after their details were recorded, to be dealt with at a later time.

CATEGORY FOUR: Those deemed useless to the Germans and therefore destined to be transported to Auschwitz and summarily exterminated. Crammed into gas chambers and murdered with poisonous gas. This category largely comprised the elderly, the sick and infirm, young children, pregnant women and new mothers.

As the Jews were scrutinised and assigned to categories, they quickly understood the meaning of the allocations and realised what was happening. In a state of panic, some tried to move from one designated area to another, to effectively change categories, but the Germans immediately shot anyone who broke ranks.

Desperate screams and cries of anguish wrung out as families were separated, never to see each other again. It was an appalling scene of misery and despair. Josh was in a state of shock and bewilderment as the horrendous scene unfolded around him, his senses overloaded by the sights and sounds of an entire community being brutally wrenched apart.

Solomon and Menasche were selected in category one and allowed to go home immediately. Josh, Bronia and Rachel were selected in category four—quite literally a death sentence. From the moment of his selection, Josh's chances of surviving the next week dropped to less than one in a thousand. He watched in stunned silence as his father and brother were ushered away, aware of his perilous position and the devastating realisation that he was unlikely to ever see them again.

Bronia, Josh and Rachel held each other tightly as they moved away from the tables towards the centre of the field. Too terrified to scream, or even speak, despair filled every cell in Josh's body.

The people assigned to category four were corralled on the soccer field, with no shelter from the elements, to await transportation to Auschwitz and their deaths. Adding to the misery, the weather turned bitterly cold and it started to rain heavily. No food or drinking water was provided and people had to make do with the remnants of whatever they had brought with them.

That night, Bronia, Josh and Rachel huddled together, shivering and terrified, as they tried to sleep on the muddy grass. They felt like caged animals: wet, cold and hungry, with no hope of escaping their certain fate.

* * *

During their second day on the field, a woman in a nurse's uniform approached Bronia. She said "I've been instructed by your husband to take Rachel out. Give her to me, this is the only way to save her." Bronia hesitated momentarily but realised that she had no choice but to trust this stranger with her precious daughter. Bronia and Josh looked on in anguished silence as the nurse took Rachel away, desperately hoping that this would be her salvation.

Josh and Bronia had no idea how Solomon had managed this miracle, rescuing baby Rachel from the clutches of the Nazis. Bronia's very core was riven with conflict between the relief of seeing Rachel seemingly taken away from imminent danger and the worry of no longer having Rachel in her care. They could only hope and pray that she would be safe.

After a second miserable night on the soccer field, the members of category four were moved to three separate locations in the centre of town. Josh and Bronia were relocated to an empty residential compound at 18 Targowa Street. This three level apartment building enclosing a quadrangle also featured a basement level and a roof space. Multiple entrances led off the quadrangle into the building.

Of the 8000 people categorised for deportation, around 2000 were crammed into the compound at 18 Targowa Street, which had been designed to accommodate less than 100 people. This was to be Josh and Bronia's home for the next few days, as the Germans arranged transport to Auschwitz. Again, no food was provided. Everyone searched desperately for ways to escape, while rumours circulated about their fate.

Josh and Bronia stayed together, moving around the overcrowded building searching for extra space but mainly spending time in the courtyard, looking out through the gates to see what was happening on the street. Bronia occasionally muttered some soothing words to Josh, but mostly they huddled together silently. No-one from their extended family was imprisoned in Targowa Street with them.

Conditions in the building were appalling. The overcrowding caused the toilets to become blocked and unusable, and the stench was unbearable. People were starving to death—particularly the old and very young—and lay motionless wherever they fell. In the crowded conditions, tripping over dead bodies was unavoidable. The mood was heavy with abject fear, distress and hopelessness.

* * *

After four wretched days in the building, Bronia was approached by two members of the Jewish police force. "We've been sent to take you out, but we will need to be rough to make it look like you are being arrested." The policemen told Bronia, in hearing shot of Josh, to pretend to resist as they roughed her up. They shoved her from one to the other as they dragged her out of the front gate. Josh watched on, disguising his inner turmoil, as his mother disappeared from view.

Now Josh was alone, tired and terrified. An eight-year-old boy all on his own in a crowd of distraught people, all too preoccupied with their own hopeless predicament to pay any attention to him.

For the remainder of that day and night, he desperately moved around the building looking for ways to escape or hide, but he could see no way out. Would someone come to take him out? Was that even possible? Would his dad be able to save him too? Or was he doomed to share the fate of those around him: a one-way trip to the gas chambers in Auschwitz. Waves of panic washed over him. He didn't sleep at all that night.

The next morning, a man approached an exhausted Josh and asked, "Are you Pila?" "Yes" responded Josh nervously. "Then follow me," said the man and turned and walked away. He did not identify himself or say another word. Josh followed the man up the stairs to the top floor of the apartment block and then through a trap door into the roof-space. They climbed through neighbouring roofs and down the steps of a nearby building. In the basement was a bakery. It was early morning and the day's bread had just come out of the oven.

Josh was directed to lie down in a horse-drawn cart used by the bakery for deliveries. Hundreds of warm, freshly baked bread loaves were then piled on top of him. Josh was on the brink of starvation so the smell of the fresh bread was incredibly sweet and the two hours he spent hidden under the bread, bouncing around in the cart, would leave a lasting impression on him for the rest of his life. Bread has remained one of his favourite foods ever since.

The horse and cart did its rounds, delivering bread to local cafes. When Josh was finally instructed to get out, he was overwhelmed to find his father, Solomon, waiting to meet him and take him home.

At home, the family was reunited. They hugged and kissed each other with tears of joy. Each excitedly told their story. Solomon explained how he was able to organise their rescue through his contacts on the Judenrat, made during his time on the Revisionist committee; Bronia described her mock arrest; and Josh recounted his daring crawl through the roof spaces and hiding in the bread cart.

About 8,000 Jews were deported to Auschwitz as part of that action. They had been selected for extermination on the soccer field so no further selection process was required on the train platform at their destination. They were murdered in the gas chambers immediately on arrival.

Eyewitness accounts describe the escape of a small number of Sosnowiec Jews who were selected in category four, always with the help of people on the outside, but there would not have been more than a handful.

* * *

Selection processes like the punkt *were undertaken throughout Poland and Nazi-occupied Europe during the course of 1942. Seventy-five percent of the three million Polish Jews murdered during the Holocaust were alive at the beginning of 1942 and dead by the end of that year.*

JOSH WITH BROTHER, MENASCHE, AND HIS MOTHER, BRONIA. ALL MANAGED TO ESCAPE THE FIRST DEPORTATION OF SOSNOWIEC JEWS TO AUSCHWITZ

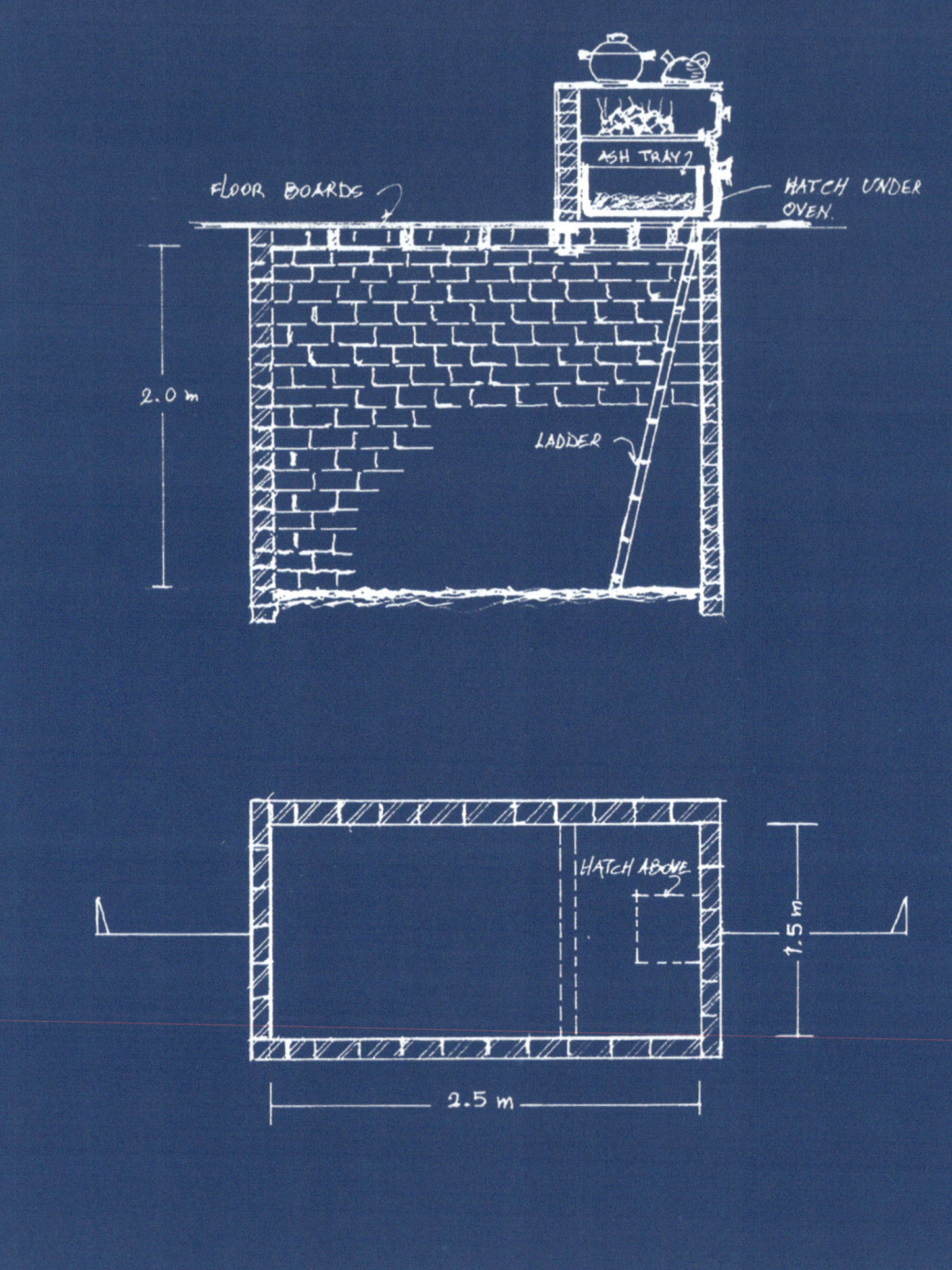

MANY DECADES AFTER ESCAPING THE GHETTO, JOSH DREW THIS DIAGRAM OF THE BUNKER WHERE HE HAD HIDDEN FROM THE NAZIS

BUNKER

Imagine not seeing daylight for the best part of eight months. Imagine spending 22 hours a day sitting in a small, dark, musty, underground space with dirt floors, no windows, no furniture, no light and no way to get out without assistance from the outside.

That was Josh's life in Srodula.

* * *

Srodula, a small, poor farming village just outside of Sosnowiec, was the site chosen by the Germans to establish a ghetto for the remaining Jews of the town. The local farmers and their families were moved out, presumably to occupy the houses and apartments from which the Jews in Sosnowiec had been forcibly evicted.

The relocation of the local Jewish population took several months. Then, in March 1943, the ghetto was closed off to the outside. Srodula was surrounded by barbed wire, eight to 10 feet high, and guard towers. Armed guards and dogs patrolled the perimeter. In May 1943, the Nazis issued orders that no Jew could leave Srodula, other than for previously approved work, and no non-Jew could enter. The Jews were completely cut off from society. Srodula had effectively become a large, high-security prison.

The ghetto had unmade roads and many of the houses had no plumbing or running water. Water had to be carried from the river or well in buckets. Food rationing tightened further. Whereas many Jews had previously been able to supplement inadequate rations with food acquired from non-Jews on the black market, this was no longer possible after the ghetto was sealed off. Starvation and diseases were rife.

Jews who had jobs in and around Sosnowiec were marched out of the main gate each morning with an armed escort and marched back at the end of the day.

* * *

Josh's family was relocated to Srodula in November 1942, a few short months after avoiding deportation during the *punkt*. The Judenrat assigned them a house in upper Srodula. They were lucky. While the houses in upper Srodula were very basic, they were luxurious compared to the barracks-style accommodation that had been newly built in lower Srodula, where the bulk of the Jewish population were housed.

The family packed their few belongings—beds, linen, clothing, food provisions, potatoes, sauerkraut, pots, pans, crockery, coal—onto a cart and wheeled it to their new home, a two-bedroom farmhouse. Before moving in, Solomon had relocated his smoking and sausage-making equipment into a standalone building in the back garden. He also took the opportunity to commence work on the bunker that was to be used as a hiding place for Josh and Rachel. Menasche did not need to be hidden as he was older and had a valid working pass, so the risk that he would be rounded up and sent to Auschwitz was significantly lower.

* * *

The fate of young Jewish children was becoming increasingly precarious. Not deemed fit for slave labour, children were considered useless by the Nazi regime and so, along with the elderly and infirm, they were the first to be designated for extermination. It was common for working parents to come home at the end of the day to find their children had been taken off the street or kidnapped from their homes and deported to the death camps.

Parents desperately sought hiding places for their young children. Sometimes they were hidden in plain sight, left in the care of a non-Jewish family, ideally with false papers that allowed them to assume a Christian identity. Non-Jewish families would take in Jewish children, either for payment, out of friendship or because they thought it was the right thing to do. Harbouring Jewish children put those families in grave danger, including the risk of death if caught.

The alternative was to physically hide children, out of sight, in specially constructed hide-outs. The term used by the Jews for such a hide-out was 'bunker'.

Many different types of bunkers were devised, each with its own advantages and disadvantages. A hidden space in the loft or roof-space of a house had the benefit that, if detected, the children might at least have a chance of escaping onto the roof and running away. Another typical hiding place was behind a false back or under a false floor in a cupboard. These spaces were very small and therefore impractical for long-term use. Underground bunkers were also common. These could comprise a hole under a barn floor or a secret space attached to the cellar. Most houses in the region had cellars for storing coal, potatoes and cabbages over the long winter months.

Constructing these hiding places became a major industry in Srodula and in ghettos throughout German-occupied Europe as the transportation and extermination of the Jews intensified.

The bunker in Josh's house in Srodula was underground. It was built by Solomon with the assistance of paid contractors who specialised in creating hiding spaces. A small section of the cellar was bricked off in a way that could not be detected by a soldier searching for hidden children. The entrance to the bunker was not through the cellar but rather through the oven in the kitchen.

The kitchen was the most important room in any farmhouse and the oven was always the centrepiece. Josh's house had a typically large coal-fired oven. It was about six feet long and three feet wide, with a top plate in which there were several rings or hot plates for cooking. The front of the oven had three doors. The two side doors had compartments where dishes could be put in for roasting or baking. The middle door had a metal plate on which the coals would be loaded for burning and a lower plate for collecting ashes. Below the lower plate was the wooden floor of the kitchen. A hinged trap door had been cut into the wooden floor below the lower plate allowing access to the bricked-off bunker below.

To enter or exit the bunker, the middle door was opened, the lower plate removed, and the trap door swung open. A permanent ladder was installed for climbing up and down. Significantly, the bunker could only be opened from above. Those inside the bunker were effectively trapped unless released by someone on the outside.

The bunker was particularly effective because it was possible to use the oven while people were hidden below. A German soldier, conducting a search for hidden children, would not be inclined to try and pull out the lower plate that was hot and covered in burning ashes.

The bunker was bounded by the supporting walls of the oven in the basement of the house. This provided a space that was around eight feet long, five-and-a-half feet wide, and about seven feet high.

The walls were brick and the floor was dirt. It had no heating, lights or electricity.

It was difficult for extended family members living in the crowded barracks of lower Srodula to create effective hiding places and so, during the first months of their stay in the ghetto, Josh and Rachel shared their hiding spot with several cousins and one of Solomon's aunts. However, over time, their cousins and great-aunt returned to their homes and were eventually all transported to Auschwitz. Towards the end of their time in Srodula, the bunker was occupied by Josh and Rachel alone.

Josh and Rachel hid in the bunker for most of the eight months that the family lived in Srodula, particularly during high risk times following rumours of an imminent action to round up Jews. One of the few times Josh left the bunker was to visit other family members in lower Srodula for Passover[16], on 19 April 1943. They had completed all of the pre-meal prayers and formalities of the Passover *seder* and finished their soup, but were yet to eat their meagre main meal, when a rumour began rapidly circulating in the ghetto that a German raid was imminent. The family abandoned the rest of the Passover meal and hurried back to their respective houses, and, in the case of Josh and Rachel, the relative safety of the bunker.

* * *

The Germans established ghettos like Srodula all over Europe. There were perhaps 1000 such ghettos in Poland and Ukraine alone. They were intended to be temporary locations to separate the Jews from the rest of society, until they could be deported to the concentration camps for extermination. The ghettos were miserable places, overcrowded and unsanitary. Starvation and disease ran rampant. People

---

16 The Jewish festival celebrating the exodus of the ancient Israelites from Egypt.

struggled for day-to-day survival but with little prospect of surviving longer term.

Ghettos were cleared progressively as Jews died of disease and starvation, were shot in the streets, or sent to death camps. Periodically, greater numbers were transported in larger 'actions'. In the Srodula ghetto, larger deportations took place in May 1943 (1000 people), June 1943 (200 people) and in August 1943 (10,000 people). This August action was intended to make Srodula 'Judenrein' (clean of Jews). Only about 1000 Jews remained to clean up the ghetto and collect any belongings that might be of value to the Germans. These last 1000 people were deported in two tranches over the following few months.

* * *

In the bunker, Josh and Rachel would sit in darkness. They were reluctant to use heavily rationed candles that used up oxygen in the badly ventilated space.

Most nights, at around 1am, Josh's parents would pull out the middle plate of the oven and open the access hole to the bunker. Josh would climb up the ladder, through the access hole, and out of the oven. If Rachel was awake, he would climb halfway up the ladder and pass Rachel to one of the parents waiting above. He was especially careful carrying this precious cargo. The house was dark but they could not risk attracting attention by lighting any candles.

Josh would look longingly out of the window at the dark street. In the moonlight, he might catch sight of a horse, a dog or a cat wandering the street. How he envied them, they were free and not burdened by unceasing threat. Then he would hop under the covers in his parents' bed where they would chat quietly. It was by far his favourite time of day. However, they would only stay out of the bunker for a couple of hours before packing some food for the next day and heading back underground.

They say that a soldier's experience of war is of long periods of abject boredom interspersed by moments of sheer terror. The same could be said about hiding in a bunker. Without light, the children could not read books or play games. There was nothing to do in the bunker but talk and try to sleep. Basic activities such as showering and brushing teeth were not possible and their toilet comprised a bucket that needed to be cleaned out each night during their brief respite above ground.

Because Bronia and Solomon worked from home they could be on the lookout for German patrols in their vicinity. Rumours circulated about when the next 'action' would take place. While Josh and Rachel remained hidden in the bunker for most of the time that the family was in Srodula, even greater care was taken when their parents believed that an 'action' was imminent. The Germans knew that people, particularly children, were being hidden in bunkers and randomly raided houses looking for hiding places.

In the bunker, Josh could hear footsteps on the kitchen floor. He quickly came to recognise the sounds of his parents' footsteps and could tell if there were different people walking above. Footsteps of soldiers in heavy boots were particularly distinctive. About once a fortnight, the children would hear a knock on the floor above the bunker, a signal that German soldiers were approaching. Other than looking for tell-tale signs of a hidden space, their most effective way of finding people was to stand quietly and listen for noises. A cough, a word, a sob, or a scrape on the wall was all that was needed to identify where people were hiding. When Josh and the others in the bunker heard the signal from above, they understood that their lives depended on their ability to remain absolutely still and quiet.

A crying baby was the most common way for a bunker to be discovered. In Srodula and other ghettos, many babies were accidentally smothered to death in an attempt to keep them quiet. Stories of such tragedies were known to Josh and his family. What would Josh do if Rachel started to cry while German soldiers were listening? This was a major source of stress in the household.

In early 1943, Rachel was not yet two years old. Josh stayed close to his baby sister during the many hours in the bunker and, when danger was nearby, he moved even closer, ready to place a hand over her mouth if she uttered the smallest sound. While not able to fully comprehend the danger they were in, somehow Rachel always knew she had to be quiet. During their many months in hiding, she had an instinctive sense for what was required. She never made a sound when the Germans were near; she never cried.

Josh's bunker stood the test of time—his hiding spot below the oven was never discovered. While life in the bunker was very uncomfortable, Josh felt safe while in hiding, particularly when compared to how vulnerable he felt at other stages of the war. In the bunker, he didn't have to worry about what to do next. He was hidden from those who wanted to do him harm and he felt protected by his parents who were always nearby and looking out for him from above like a pair of guardian angels.

ESCAPE

"Nie pchai sie jak Zyd—Don't push like a Jew," the tram conductress snarled at Josh in Polish. Josh froze momentarily. He was terrified that someone might identify him as a Jew and desperately tried to avoid attracting any attention. Particularly so now, when he was on an important mission and carrying a sizeable sum of money.

* * *

After Srodula had been substantially cleared of Jews in early August 1943, it was apparent that remaining in the bunker was no longer viable. Josh and Rachel were not officially living in Srodula and had no entitlement to food rations. More significantly, as the bunker could only be opened from the outside, if Josh's parents and brother were killed or deported, Josh and Rachel would have been left to starve to death in the dark. The time to leave the bunker was fast approaching.

The family made the courageous decision to attempt to escape from Srodula, which was still under armed guard. It meant surviving on the outside with no home, no food coupons and no identity papers. They would have to exist amongst a hostile population with the ever-present risk that if their Jewish identity was exposed, they would be killed or deported. The challenges were seemingly insurmountable, but they had no other options. If they remained in

SRODULO GHETTO WHERE JOSH AND HIS FAMILY LIVED UNTIL THEY ESCAPED, SHORTLY BEFORE THE GHETTO WAS LIQUIDATED

Srodula, they would either die of starvation or be transported to an extermination camp.

Solomon made plans for their escape and put in place arrangements on the outside. While Josh was not aware what influence or contacts Solomon had, it is most likely that the German official from the Sosnowiec police station was involved.

The first step in their escape was to smuggle Josh out of Srodula to a contact in another town. Nine-year-old Josh was to be the 'canary in the coal mine', beating a path that the others would follow if he were successful. Josh was chosen by his parents to go first as he had already proven himself to be street smart and resourceful. He had the attributes and attitude to survive on his own. He was also considered by everyone in his family to be the 'lucky one'.

While he felt some trepidation about leaving the protection of his parents, Josh was positive and optimistic about the idea of escaping and mostly was excited to be getting out of the bunker. He knew that the risks were immense but thought that any danger that he encountered outside the ghetto had to be preferable to sitting in the dark and claustrophobic bunker waiting to be caught.

On the appointed day in September 1943, Josh was introduced to the Jewish 'guide' who had been paid by Solomon to help him escape. He was a short man in his twenties. He briefed Josh on how they would crawl through the barbed wire and then, while keeping low to the ground, quickly run up the hill and down the other side, to the left, where they were to hide in the long grass and wait for each other. The guide cautioned him to follow his instructions without hesitation. Also coming with them was a girl of about 17, tall, dark-haired and attractive.

They headed off late one afternoon along *Ziegenweg*—Goat's Way, the street the family lived on—hugging the buildings and trying to stay invisible. *Ziegenweg* was less than 100 metres long and ran uphill toward the barbed wire fence that surrounded the ghetto.

The upper ghetto, which comprised a series of streets set out in a grid, was largely deserted. Most of the remaining Jews in Srodula were in the lower ghetto and the few still in the upper ghetto were not out on the streets. It was virtually a ghost town.

Soon the trio came within sight of the fence. It loomed about 10-feet high, with razor sharp barbs glistening in the late afternoon sun. Wooden guard boxes at regular intervals punctuated the perimeter. Josh had seen the fence before, of course, but now he viewed it in a new light. How were they supposed to get through it?

As they got closer, Josh could see a hole cut in the fence; the guide had clearly used this route before. They were to climb through the hole one at a time as the guide looked out for guards.

As directed, Josh scrambled through the hole first while the guide and the girl stood back behind a nearby house to remain hidden. He could feel his heart racing, adrenaline surging through his body. He felt much older than his nine years, like a soldier on a daring mission. It felt good. He felt alive.

Josh had to move slowly and carefully through the wire to avoid being caught on the sharp barbs. At the same time, he could not afford to linger a moment longer than was necessary. As he climbed through the hole, he was completely exposed and if the guards saw him, they would shoot him immediately.

Once through the hole, Josh hurried to the top of the hill as fast as he could and then down to the designated meeting point. The girl followed next with the guide bringing up the rear, with Josh watching their every move. The three waited a few moments to allow their accelerated heart rates to settle. They took deep breaths; the air seemed so much clearer and fresher than the air in the ghetto. Josh felt liberated and elated, focused and alert. He was hyper aware of every detail around him. The trio were only a few hundred meters from the ghetto, but everything seemed so different. Josh no longer felt like a caged animal.

One of the advantages of escaping after most of the ghetto had been cleared and only a skeleton crew of prisoners remained, was that it was far less heavily guarded. Also, the guards in the upper part of the ghetto were Romanian. The Romanian guards were less engaged and attentive to their duties than their German allies; essentially, they just went through the motions so it was easier to predict when they would be doing their rounds and therefore escape without being noticed. To Josh's great relief, they exited the ghetto without even seeing a guard.

The best way to put some distance between themselves and the ghetto was to board a tram towards Sosnowiec. It would have only taken a few minutes to follow the fence down the hill to the nearest tram stop, but that stop was located right outside a German police station. Instead, they scampered down the other side of the hill and across the fields towards the light railway line on the main road between Bedzin and Sosnowiec. Bedzin is a 15-minute tram ride away from Sosnowiec, on a tramway system that serviced a dozen or so towns in the Zaglembie and Upper Silesia region. Over the coming period, Josh would use the tram system extensively and develop intimate knowledge of the timetables, stops and pricing of trips. Even at his young age, he had to do so without asking for directions and without ever appearing to be unsure of what he was doing.

When the next tram to Sosnowiec arrived, they jumped on and paid the conductor. Josh felt like everyone on the tram was looking at them. He was painfully aware of even the most casual glance in his direction from any of the other passengers. Although sick to the stomach with fear, the three of them pretended not to be nervous and concentrated hard on acting naturally and blending in with the crowd.

They were outside the ghetto and away from the guards but by no means safe. At any time, they could have been arrested by German or Polish authorities and immediately deported to a death camp. If anyone even suspected that they were Jewish, their lives would be in great peril. The stakes could not have been higher.

By now it was getting late and they needed somewhere to stay the night in Sosnowiec. The guide knocked on the door of a house belonging to someone he knew. A woman opened the door, looked quickly up and down the street, and then hustled the trio inside and into a bedroom, wanting to get them out of sight as quickly as possible.

Lying on the floor with a blanket, Josh felt much more comfortable than he had been in the bunker. He was exhausted from his nerve-wracking escape earlier in the day and, out of sight in the dark, with the curtains closed, he felt relatively safe. Still, Josh was away from his parents, with strangers in a cold and hostile world, and he remained alert to every sound.

The next day, Josh and the guide left the teenage girl in Sosnowiec and took a tram to Katowitz and another tram to Koenigshutte, each a 20-minute journey. The guide was very business-like, giving Josh instructions but not engaging in any small talk. Josh just focused on keeping up with his adult companion.

The guide delivered Josh to Solomon's contact in Koenigshutte. He was a man in his forties, of medium height and build with hair receding from his high forehead. He owned a fancy shop selling cheeses, butter and other dairy products. This man had been paid by Solomon to help his family but in doing so, he had put his own life at risk.

Josh stayed with the dairy shop owner for a few weeks, living in the house behind the shop and sharing meals with him and his wife; they either didn't have children or their children no longer lived at home. Eating meals at a table, rather than in the musky darkness of the bunker, was a welcome change. The couple were very nice to Josh, always treating him well, but never asking him questions about his family or his experiences thus far during the war.

The plan was for Josh to live in the open pretending to be Catholic. The dairy shop owner taught Josh religious prayers, in German, and customs, including the Catholic bedtime prayers, so important for maintaining his cover as a Catholic boy.

He showed Josh around the town and instructed him in how to use coupons to buy food at the butcher, bread shop, milk shop and grocery store. It was important that Josh looked like he knew what he was doing when shopping with coupons—any hesitation or misstep could blow his cover with fatal consequences.

Josh's new guardian also organised a Hitler youth badge for him, a small token that he wore on his chest. The Hitler youth badge came with a piece of paper identifying his name. It was not an official identity document but it was better than having no documents whatsoever. The paper that came with the badge identified Josh as 'Johannes', or 'Hans'. This was to be his name—other than during very private moments with his family—for the next year and a half. Josh quite liked the name Hans and got used to it quickly.

Josh would only leave the house when told to by the dairy shop owner. At first, they would go out together, but soon Josh earned his trust and he would be sent out on his own to run errands or buy supplies.

Shopping with individual coupons was suspicious as 'legitimate' citizens were expected to bring their whole coupon card to the store when collecting rations. Only someone who had not been allocated a card—those who had escaped the camps or ghettos or were living under a false identity—would use detached coupons. The exception were children sent to the shops with individual coupons to minimise the risk of losing the whole monthly ration card. This allowed young Josh to trade detached coupons without raising undue suspicion.

* * *

Josh expected Bronia and Rachel to join him about one week after he had left the ghetto. However, after several weeks they still had not arrived. He had no way of knowing what had happened. Maybe they had not been able to escape the ghetto. Maybe they had left the ghetto but had been caught on the way to find him. He had no idea what to do and, as the weeks dragged by, he became increasingly anxious. The dairy shop owner just shrugged his shoulders; he didn't know either.

Josh and the dairy shop owner agreed that he would have to return to Srodula to find out what was happening. He retraced his steps back to the ghetto, taking the three trams to the stop on the Sosnowiec/Bedzin road. He walked carefully through the fields and up the hill, checked for guards and then slipped through the hole in the fence. The route was familiar but no less dangerous than before. He was effectively breaking back into a jail and he felt the same surge of adrenaline as when he first escaped.

Very soon Josh was back in his home with his family. They were shocked but overjoyed to see him. Bronia cried with relief. When he had left, no-one had known if they would ever be together again. Now he was back, full of stories about the dairy shop and life on the outside. A brief moment of celebration for the family, like a momentary ray of sunshine during a heavy, unrelenting storm.

Bronia explained that she'd had to delay her departure from the ghetto because she had fallen ill with a kidney infection. Nursing abdominal pain and a high fever, she had no access to medication or medical attention. Also, the guide that had taken Josh out of the ghetto had decided that his 'business' had become too dangerous and he was no longer available to assist. Without him, Bronia had not known how to escape.

Of course, Srodula was still not safe for Josh. The ghetto had been cleared of Jews, other than a few workers, and the presence of any children would certainly look conspicuous. Josh and Rachel were again banished to the tedium of the bunker, where they spent the next couple of weeks. Rachel was particularly happy to have Josh return. They had grown very close during their many hours in hiding and she hated being in the bunker without him. As before, Josh and Rachel sat in the dark together, listening to the footsteps above, waiting for the signal warning them that the Nazi hunting-parties were approaching.

Finally, a couple of weeks later, towards the end of October, Solomon and Bronia decided that it was time for Josh, Bronia and Rachel to leave the ghetto. As they were leaving for good, they packed a few items. They could only take a small bag each; it would look suspicious to walk the streets and ride the trams with suitcases or large bags. What they carried with them would comprise their worldly possessions—although given their previous moves, they didn't have much to leave behind.

They needed to take warm clothes as they were heading into winter, but avoid any garments that could identify them as Jewish. This meant ensuring that none of their clothes left a shadow from the Star of David badges they had been wearing. In effect, they had to choose clothing that had not been worn in recent years and so never had the badges affixed. It also meant discarding any clothes identifiable as popular Jewish fashion, such as coats made from the fur of unborn sheep. To keep their baggage to a minimum, they each wore as many items as they could, including several shirts and several pairs of socks.

They took food to eat, including extra sausage which would be a valuable currency on the outside. They did not take any photos or identity papers that could potentially be incriminating. Rachel did not have any toys but she did have a small, multi-coloured security blanket that she liked to chew on.

This time Josh would be the guide for Bronia and Rachel, an enormous responsibility given the high stakes. They took the same route out of the ghetto, passing Rachel between them through the hole in the barbed wire fence. This had to be managed with great care and Rachel, although barely two years old, knew to be very still. It did mean that all three of them had to be at the fence together, increasing their risk of being detected by the guards.

Once through, they walked to the tram stop to embark on their three-tram journey. It was a difficult trip as Bronia had to carry Rachel the whole way. Finally, they made it to Koenigshutte and the home of the dairy shop owner, whom Bronia seemed to know.

Once again, Josh assumed the name Hans and Rachel was given the name 'Christina' or 'Kusha'. They established a cover story in which Bronia was the aunt of Josh and Rachel, looking after them because their father was a soldier on the Eastern front and their mother was very sick.

During this time, Bronia travelled around the local towns, by foot or tram, looking for cleaning jobs. As their 'aunt' who had been unexpectedly left with custody of the children, if she was unable to find somewhere to leave them for short stays, she would bring Josh and Rachel with her.

* * *

Several weeks later, in late November 1943, Bronia told Josh to go to Sosnowiec to meet Solomon and collect more money to give to the dairy shop owner. The plan was for Solomon to meet a man, who was going to take over his smallgoods factory, at the market on Dekerta Street. Solomon was to be escorted to the market by a German official, the same official who had visited their house on occasion, and would be able to pass money to Josh.

JOSH TRAVELLED FROM TOWN TO TOWN ON THE LOCAL TRAM NETWORK TO AVOID STAYING IN ONE PLACE LONG ENOUGH TO AROUSE SUSPICION

It was bitterly cold when Josh arrived at the designated meeting spot at about 10 in the morning. It was disconcerting to return to the Jewish heart of Sosnowiec, so close to the remains of the old synagogue, now entirely devoid of Jewish people. He felt unsafe and exposed and was worried that someone might recognise him. He did not want to be there a moment longer than necessary.

Josh tried to fade into the background. Rather than entering the market, he stood in a doorway, across the road, where he had a good view of the market entrance, but could easily get away at the first sign of trouble. He did not want to be noticed or questioned as to what he was doing there or why he was not at school. He did not want to stand out in any way.

The appointed hour came and went but Solomon did not arrive for the meeting.

There must have been a change of plan regarding the factory handover.

Josh waited for four or five hours until it became clear that Solomon wasn't coming at all. Again, Josh was desperately worried and in a terrible dilemma. Had something happened to his father? Could he go back to his mother empty-handed? They needed the money, what would happen if the dairy shop owner did not get paid? Should he risk yet another trip back to the ghetto? There were no good options and no-one with whom he could discuss his predicament. The enormous decision fell heavily on his small shoulders.

His mind raced as he contemplated his options. Finally, Josh decided that he would re-enter the lions' den and return once again to Srodula. He knew how to breach the fence and slip into the ghetto, and with the bravado of youth, he was confident that he could return without getting caught.

In addition to avoiding the guards, he was careful not to be seen by other residents of Srodula. This was not difficult as the ghetto was even more sparsely populated than before. When he arrived at his old house, he found Menasche in the room behind the kitchen. His brother was stunned to see Josh and gawked at him incredulously, as if he were seeing a ghost. Once Menasche recovered, he raced to get their father from the factory in the backyard. Solomon ran to the house and looked at Josh with wide eyes and a dropping jaw. "Are you crazy? What are you doing here?", he blurted out in disbelief. They all embraced.

Solomon and Menasche were both shocked and excited to see Josh, but worried about the dangers that he was exposed to. Having missed the meeting at the market in Sosnowiec, due to a last minute change of plans by the German official, Solomon was particularly relieved to be able to give Josh the money needed to pass on to the dairy shop owner.

The Germans could round up the final few hundred Jews remaining in Srodula at any time; it was an incredibly dangerous place for Josh. Still, the men of the family were able to spend some time at the kitchen table exchanging stories. Menasche gave Josh a piece of chocolate which he devoured straight away (he would remember the wonderful taste of that chocolate for the rest of his life) and some Hannukah gelt[17] which Josh put in his pocket.

Solomon became serious and looked his two boys in the eyes. It was a sombre moment. They were all aware that the time in the ghetto was fast coming to an end and that a new, critical stage in their quest for survival was approaching. Solomon spoke to them, father to son, man to man, with brutal honesty and no false optimism. The boys listened in stunned silence.

"It is very unlikely that any of us will survive," his father said solemnly, "but to have any chance, you need to keep a low profile. And if you do survive, do not stay on this land soaked with Jewish blood—go to Palestine…" Solomon remained an ardent Zionist to the end.

Solomon was telling his sons that he could not protect them. It was an incredibly difficult message for a parent to give and for a child to receive. The weight of his words dragged on each of their souls.

* * *

After a few precious hours together, it was time for Josh to leave. Bronia would be worried, he needed to get back to her. Solomon and Menasche could not go with him, their absence would be noticed by the German authorities and soldiers would come looking for them.

Solomon gave Josh 8000 reichmarks to hand over to Bronia, a very large sum of money, 30 to 40 times a worker's basic monthly wage. Solomon wrapped the notes into a scarf and tied it around Josh's chest, under his shirt. Solomon also gave Josh some reichmarks for

---

17 It was traditional to give small sums of money to mark the Jewish festival of Hannukah which fell at that time.

himself. Josh would need to be very careful with this money: he had to make it last.

Josh left the ghetto for the last time by his usual route. In one flat section of the field, Josh was concerned that his dark clothing on the white snow background made him too visible. To reduce his exposure, Josh crawled through the cold, wet snow. It was slow work, his clothing became soaked through and his hands ached from the bitter cold, but at least he wasn't noticed by the guards.

Josh took the tram to Sosnowiec and there he waited for the tram to Katowitz. When it arrived at the Sosnowiec terminus, Josh was anxious to climb aboard and did not wait until other passengers had disembarked and the tram had turned around.

"Don't push like a Jew," the conductress snarled at Josh in Polish. The hairs on Josh's neck stood on end. Out in public he was always on edge, but he was particularly tense now knowing that under his clothes he held a fortune in reichmarks, money that was critical to the survival of his family.

He felt trapped and the emotions of the long and challenging day boiled to the surface. Josh, a small, slight, nine-year-old boy, turned to the conductress, glared at her and snapped *"Du Polnische schwein, du must ja nur Deutsch sprechen—*You Polish swine, you must speak only German."

In occupied Silesia, only *volksdeutche* (ethnically German people) could get public service jobs, such as in a post office or as a tram conductor, and they were required to speak German. To speak Polish was a serious offence that could cost them their job—or worse.

The tram conductress turned white and started shaking. The tables had turned. From then on, she stayed as far away from Josh as she could. No other passenger on the tram said a word, made a sound, or caught Josh's eye for the remainder of the trip to Katowitz. Now, they were afraid of him. In an atmosphere of persistent fear, even a small boy was a threat, someone who could report them to the authorities and put them in grave danger. Everyone had something to hide.

Josh was unable to enjoy this unexpected power. His father had just told him the importance of keeping a low profile, and here he was doing exactly the opposite. He was ashamed and churning inside, desperately frightened but unable to show it. The tram ride seemed to take forever—15 minutes felt like hours—before the tram finally reached his stop. He jumped off as soon as he could and ran to the next tram to Koenigshutte.

Finally, he was back at the dairy shop. Bronia had been beside herself with worry, fearing that he had been caught. She had expected him back at midday and it was now 9pm in the evening, dark and freezing. Bronia ushered him into a quiet room, hugged him and sat him down. Josh lifted his shirt, untied the scarf and handed her the money that Solomon had sent. Some of this money she set aside to give to the dairy shop owner; the balance she carefully hid in her clothing. This money was their lifeline.

Bronia asked about Solomon and Menasche. They spoke quietly into the night—about the ghetto, about when Solomon and Menasche might join them, about his father's solemn words and, most importantly, about how they would get through the next day.

SOLOMON PROUDLY WEARING THE UNIFORM
OF THE REVISIONISTS

ON THE OUTSIDE

By the end of December 1943, Josh and his immediate family had all left the Srodula ghetto and were living in the broader non-Jewish community.

Their escape from Srodula was timely. By January 1944, the last remaining Jews were transported to Auschwitz and the ghetto was liquidated. Most of the Jews sent from Srodula to the extermination camp were murdered in the gas chambers immediately on arrival. The 'lucky' few, those deemed fit for slave labour, remained alive as inmates of Auschwitz—a living hell of deprivation, starvation, disease and cruelty, with death around every corner. Had they been deported to Auschwitz, Josh and Rachel would have been considered too young to be useful and would have been killed the same day.

For the time being, Josh's family had escaped the fate of so many friends and relatives. But now a new phase in their quest for survival was to begin. During this phase, lasting just over a year, Josh would stay at 38 different addresses, battle several childhood diseases, lose half his family and experience moments of incredible luck and deep despair.

The Battle of Stalingrad, won by the Russians in early 1943, was one of the great turning points of World War II. From that time, Germany was on the defensive across the entire Eastern theatre. Russian armies advanced across a huge front that spanned the European peninsula from north to south. By the end of 1943, they had liberated Kiev and Smolensk and occupied a large part of the Ukraine. The Russians intended to march all the way to Berlin, with Silesia well and truly in their path.

* * *

With the slow advance of the Russian army, survival for Josh and his family was a day-by-day proposition. Every minute, every hour and every day they stayed out of the Nazis' clutches brought them a minute, an hour, a day, closer to salvation. They nonetheless feared that it was only a matter of time until they were caught. As careful and clever as they were, eventually their luck would surely run out.

It had become clear, from reading newspapers, that Germany was losing the war; however there was nothing Josh's family could do to hasten the inevitable outcome, that was up to others. All they could do was try to remain alive and free for as long as possible. It was a race against the clock to hold on until the Germans conceded defeat or the Russian army arrived.

* * *

A small number of European Jews survived the Holocaust in different ways.

Some managed to escape from the German-occupied territories to see out the war in places such as Siberia, China or South America. Others sought the safety of neutral countries such as Switzerland or Sweden. However, by late 1943, borders were tightly closed to any such emigration. Jews needed special permits even to leave the local region. There was nowhere to go and no way to get there.

Some Jews were sent to labour camps and death camps and survived against the odds.

Some managed to acquire fake identity documents that allowed them to live in the community while concealing their Jewish identities. False papers were extremely hard to come by and required the services of expert forgers. In some cases, priests helped Jews by issuing them a false certificate of baptism. This certificate could then be used to acquire 'legitimate' identity papers.

In rural areas, some escaped to the forests and joined partisan groups, using guerrilla warfare tactics to fight the Nazis.

Others were taken in by non-Jews, often for payment, and spent the war in hiding. For children, this sometimes meant hiding in plain sight, where the Christian family would pretend that the child was their own. Many such deceptions were exposed, with deadly consequences for both the Jewish child and the family who tried to protect them.

Josh's experiences did not fit into any of those categories.

* * *

The challenges facing Jews trying to live on the outside[18] and blend into the non-Jewish community were enormous.

Firstly, the Germans were meticulous record keepers. Everyone living in territories occupied by the Germans needed to be registered and hold identity papers. Without identity papers, they did not officially exist and had no entitlement to food coupons, so essential to daily subsistence. Further, any official, even a minor bureaucrat, could demand to see identity papers at any time. If someone was unable to produce them immediately, they could be arrested on the spot.

---

18 For a Jew, not being in a ghetto or concentration camp, or other place where Jews were collected, meant living 'on the outside'.

Secondly, the Jews in Eastern Europe were not well integrated into the mainstream community. While they were sometimes tolerated, they were not generally accepted and so led separate, parallel lives to their non-Jewish neighbours. They spoke their own language, Yiddish, and maintained their own culture and customs. While a Polish Jew would know how to speak Polish, they might do so with a different accent or with a smattering of words that were distinctively Yiddish. On many occasions, the true identity of a Jew masquerading as a Christian was exposed with the utterance of an indiscreet word or phrase.

Thirdly, all Jewish males were circumcised, which was not the case in the non-Jewish population, which made it immeasurably harder to hide a boy on the outside than to hide a girl.

Fourthly, Nazi authorities known as 'gauleiters' were appointed to most neighbourhoods to monitor citizens' behaviour and report any unusual or suspicious activity. Jews attempting to live on the outside were at constant risk of being discovered by the all-knowing, all-seeing gauleiters.

Finally, age-old anti-Semitism continued to thrive in the community. Most non-Jews were disinclined to help their Jewish neighbours and many would happily turn in any Jews they discovered. A non-Jew could expect a monetary reward for reporting a Jew. On the other hand, they could be severely punished, even killed, for helping a Jew.

For all these reasons, the odds were heavily stacked against any Jewish people attempting to survive on the outside. To overcome these odds required careful planning, resourcefulness, vigilance and an enormous amount of luck.

* * *

Fear is a primitive human emotion. Its evolutionary purpose is to improve the prospects of survival by injecting a person with the biological tools to aid an immediate fight or flight response. This short-term response is designed to address an immediate threat, and to dissipate once safety is achieved. Humans are not designed to sustain prolonged fear. It wraps its cold hand around the heart and squeezes, leaving the person short of breath and in a state of high anxiety. In the extreme, fear has the capacity to overwhelm the individual, suffocate rational thought, crowding out other emotions.

For most of the war, and certainly during the last year of the German occupation, Josh lived in an unrelenting state of fear. It permeated every moment of the day and night. The ever-present threat to his survival was extreme. There was not a moment when he was not in danger. This permanent state of fear heightened all of Josh's senses. He was always on alert. He could smell, hear or feel danger—even in his sleep.

Every one of the hundreds of minor decisions made every day—where to walk, what to eat, where to sleep, which corner to turn—was laced with danger. Any wrong decision, any slight misstep or misjudgement, could be fatal. And yet there was no way to know, other than with hindsight, what the right decisions were.

This was where aspects of Josh's personality came to the fore. Even at the age of nine, he was decisive, confident, disciplined and careful. He did not dwell on situations or second guess himself. He was driven by pragmatism rather than emotion and his analytical mind allowed him to assess every situation coolly and methodically. It never occurred to Josh to give up or concede defeat. As long as he was alive there was hope and everything he did was directed at staying alive. He wasted no time thinking about the past or dreaming about the future when the nightmare might end. He lived in the moment, looking only to the near-term horizon.

Despite his persistent state of dread and fear, Josh had to maintain a calm and relaxed exterior at all times. To display even momentary anxiety or uncertainty could arouse suspicion. His external appearance had to be ordinary, unexceptional, non-descript. Better yet, he needed to be invisible.

* * *

It was not an option for the family to all stay at the dairy shop owner's house for long as their presence could arouse suspicion amongst his neighbours. Solomon and Bronia decided that the best approach would be to split the family up and 'place' the family members with different people for short stints. Rachel, who was still a toddler, would stay with Bronia; Solomon would be with Menasche; and Josh would be on his own. Although Josh was younger than Menasche, he had proven over the recent months that he had the necessary street smarts and gumption to cope by himself. Josh did not question or argue against this decision, he knew it made sense.

In December 1943, Josh was billeted with a pair of unmarried sisters who lived in a basement apartment in Koenigshutte. They were both in their late forties with greying hair. To Josh they appeared ancient. The sisters were paid to have Josh live with them and were told that he needed somewhere to stay because his mother was very sick and his father was fighting on the Eastern front. They knew Josh as Hans and were never told that he was Jewish.

Life with the sisters was relatively pleasant. They were nice enough, treated Josh well, and they ate dinner together most nights—mostly Silesian food: potatoes, cabbages and soup. There was very little conversation at the dinner table, they did not ask Josh any questions about his family. During the day, Josh would run errands and do the shopping while the sisters were at work. In the morning, they would leave him a shopping list along with coupons and money.

The sisters were Catholic and very religious. Josh would join them in saying prayers before and after every meal and he would kneel in prayer at his bedside each night before going to sleep. On Sundays he went to church with them; Josh knew all the Catholic prayers and how to navigate his way around a church service automatically and without hesitation. Reciting Catholic prayers never bothered him. In fact, he often wished that he was actually Catholic so that he would not have to pretend; he envied others in church who did not have to put on a façade.

For about six weeks, Josh assumed this family life, although, bizarrely, with complete strangers in a Catholic household. He even shared Christmas with the sisters in 1943, with a Christmas tree adorning their apartment, albeit with no presents underneath.

Every two weeks, at an appointed time, Josh would briefly meet with Solomon at a pre-agreed location, often at a nearby park, where the open spaces would allow them to talk without being overheard. Josh very much looked forward to these meetings. Occasionally, Menasche would also come along. This was their chance to catch up on what they had all been doing and to finetune their strategies for survival. At the end of each meeting, they would make arrangements for their next.

Solomon and Menasche described to Josh their final few weeks in the Srodula ghetto. They had hidden for several days in someone else's bunker, at a house further up the street on the same side of the road, while the Germans continued to systematically clear out the Jews. They couldn't use the bunker where Josh and Rachel had hidden as the space could only be opened from the outside.

Menasche told Josh that on the outside, he and Solomon had been sleeping in a hiding place in a barn, together with farm animals. Bronia never came to these meetings and Josh did not know where she and Rachel were. Josh could only hear news about his mother and sister relayed through Solomon, who met them separately. The family was held together by the thinnest of threads.

* * *

Then, disaster struck!

One day in late February, Solomon failed to show up for a planned meeting. Josh waited as long as possible at the designated place as dread filled his heart. What had happened? Over the next couple of days, Josh went back to the meeting place a few more times, hoping beyond hope that his father would be there.

Josh could not go to Solomon, as he had done in the ghetto, because he had no idea where his father was. Something must have happened. What did that mean for the family's plan and for Josh's arrangements? Had the dairy shop owner sold them out or had he himself been compromised and arrested?

Josh's predicament soon became much worse. One evening, a few days later, he overheard the sisters talking about him while he pretended to be asleep. "Who do you think he really is? Maybe we should check him out, look at him a bit more closely," one of the ladies said to the other.

Josh knew exactly what this meant. They were questioning the story they had been told and contemplating checking whether he was circumcised, a quick and certain way of determining if he was Jewish. Perhaps the money from the dairy shop owner had dried up. Josh didn't sleep at all, he spent the whole night fretting about what he should do. He was in danger and needed to flee.

The next morning, the sisters left for work without leaving a shopping list or the key to the door as they usually would so that he could come and go as he pleased. Josh was locked in with no way to escape. Because the apartment was a half basement, below street level, the only windows were up high and had iron bars. There was no way out.

Josh was convinced that the sisters planned to report him to the authorities and he would be arrested. He spent the entire day frantic and distressed, like a caged animal, intermittently crying and praying to every god he could think of. He packed his few belongings and a Christian prayer book in a bag, ready to take any chance to escape.

When he heard the sisters arriving home that evening, he waited by the door, not sure if they would be accompanied by the police or Nazi soldiers. Thankfully, they were alone. As soon as the door opened, Josh dashed past the sisters and out onto the street, sprinting away without saying a word.

Being winter, it was already dark outside. Arms pumping and lungs straining, Josh ran as fast as he could into the blackness of the night. He never looked back.

BRONIA & JOSH

ALONE

It was late February 1944 and Josh was truly alone.

The fate of his father and brother was unknown. Presumably, they had been arrested. He had no idea where his mother and sister were. Only his father knew the location of each family member and now that connection was severed, the frail structure that had held their family together had collapsed. Perhaps the dairy shop owner knew more, but Josh did not dare go near him, for fear that he had been compromised or, worse, that he had betrayed the family. There were too many unknowns for him to contemplate. No-one knew where he was and there was no-one to help or guide him.

When he ran from the sisters' apartment, he did not have anywhere to go; he just knew that he had to get away. He needed to put distance between himself and the sisters and anyone else in the dairy shop owner's network. He had to leave town. Josh jumped onto the first available tram and disappeared into the night.

As he sat on the tram and looked out the window at the dark streets, he worked hard to stop his mind from racing. To acknowledge and fully contemplate his predicament would overwhelm him. Even at this most desperate of times, Josh could not afford to let his guard down. To in any way display the dread and terror that he felt inside would have drawn suspicion from the strangers around him.

He could not count on any sympathy or compassion from these fellow human beings. He willed himself to maintain a calm and composed demeanour.

Josh was a nine-year-old boy adrift in a shark-infested sea. Like a sailor who has jumped off a burning ship into the deep ocean to escape the flames, all he could do was tread water for as long as he was able.

* * *

By the end of February 1944, the Soviet army had liberated Leningrad and the surrounding region. In March 1944, they crossed the Dniester River, beginning the liberation of Moldova, and advanced to the Romanian border. The once mighty German army was being pushed towards the West. The Soviet advance was unstoppable, but they were still hundreds of kilometres from Silesia.

* * *

For the next few weeks, Josh lived the life of a homeless fugitive. He was, quite literally, an outlaw, with no legal or civil rights. None of the facilities or institutions that societies establish to provide care for children were available to him. No-one in the community cared if he lived or died. At best he encountered indifference, at worst he was surrounded by those actively seeking his eradication.

As bad as things were, Josh never considered giving up, he remained determined to survive for as long as he could. He focused on getting through one hour, one day, at a time. His concept of the future was the remainder of the day, anything beyond that was too fanciful to contemplate.

Josh had two priorities. One was to stay on the move, using trams to continuously travel between different towns. In this way, even if a person noticed him and momentarily wondered who he was and why he was on the streets instead of at home or in school, he would soon be out of sight and out of mind. His second priority was to find his parents and siblings. As he moved from place to place, his eyes scoured the streets for any sign of his family. This strategy had an extremely low likelihood of success, but it was the only thing he could do.

Fortunately, he still had some of the reichsmarks given to him by his father and brother. This money was a life saver. With no coupons, Josh was not able to buy food at the shops. However, once a day, he would go to a cheap restaurant and buy an inexpensive bowl of *zur* soup, traditional Silesian soup made from fermented stale rye bread, served with a piece of bread.

Most days he would also go to a cinema and watch a movie. Cinema tickets for children were cheap and sitting watching a movie gave him a couple of hours of respite. The cinemas were warm and sheltered, and, best of all, the darkness meant that he did not have to worry about prying eyes. On the streets, Josh was on guard every moment. In the darkness of the cinema, he felt relatively safe and anonymous. He was still very much on edge, but the movies provided a welcome distraction.

Often, he would see several movies during a day, moving to different cinemas in different towns to avoid suspicion. He became adept at navigating Silesia's extensive light rail system, and the next town was never more than a 20-minute ride away.

As the cinema lights dimmed and the screen came to life, Josh was transported to another world, a much better world. The world of Kasperl and Sepperl.

Kasperl is a famous German puppet show character with roots dating back to the 17th century. He is the perennial, unbeatable hero of German puppet theatre. He is smart, witty and brave, and he jokes and laughs in the face of danger. Sepperl is his sidekick. Together they tackle and defeat all their foes. In their world, the good guys are unflinchingly good, and the bad guys are unambiguously evil. And, at the end of the day, the good guys always win.

A series of children's movies starring these heroic puppets were being shown in cinemas throughout Silesia during early 1944. In those dark and desperate days, Josh longed for the simplicity of the world of Kasperl and Sepperl, where good always triumphed over evil, and where the downtrodden and persecuted could count on the hero to save the day.[19]

[LEFT] KASPERL WAS A FAMOUS PUPPET SHOW CHARACTER WHO ALWAYS TRIUMPHED OVER EVIL. [RIGHT] KASPERL'S SIDEKICK SEPPERL, DRAWN BY JOSH 75 YEARS AFTER THEY HELPED KEEP HIM COMPANY DURING A BITTER SILESIAN WINTER

---

19 Josh developed a lifelong love of puppets. When he became a young father, he would make his own puppet theatres and put on shows for his kids.

The bitterly cold Silesian winter nights were Josh's biggest problem. The ground was frozen solid and covered with snow. Finding shelter was a major challenge so he slept in parks and under bridges. Actual sleep was largely elusive; he was cold, uncomfortable and too on edge to close his eyes.

The situation was not sustainable. The little money he had could not last and there was no way to get more. In any event, it was only a matter of time before someone became suspicious that he was Jewish.

While he was able to use public toilets, he had no access to bathing facilities and he and his clothes were filthy. To make matters worse—though not surprising given the conditions—Josh became sick, very sick. He contracted, in quick succession, whooping cough, measles and chicken pox. For all these illnesses, the recommended treatment involves bed rest, good nutrition, hydration, a visit to the doctor and lots of parental care. None of this was available to Josh. He was fortunate not to have suffered severe complications that can come from not adequately treating these conditions.

With his health deteriorating, his energy levels depleting and his money running out, there was only so long that Josh could tread water before slipping beneath the waves and drowning. There was nothing for Josh to do but to get through each day, survive another freezing night, and see what the next day would bring.

* * *

In mid-March 1944, as the long, cold winter was finally drawing to a close, and after Josh had spent close to three weeks on his own, one of those next days brought a miracle!

Walking down the street in the town of Bismarckhutte, Josh noticed a lady coming towards him carrying a small child. In profile and gait she resembled his mother. Josh caught his breath and his heart started to race: could this be Bronia and Rachel? It was hard to be sure as the woman was rugged up against the cold and the climate of fear was such that Josh didn't dare to look at her too closely, to catch her eye or to show any hint of recognition. She clearly felt the same. The two walked right past each other without uttering a word.

They each walked another 30 paces or so before tentatively turning around to look back. That simultaneous act was all the confirmation they needed. Against all odds, a mother and her nine-year-old son had found each other. They reunited with an embrace, conscious not to raise suspicion by being overly demonstrative in the middle of the street. Even at this most euphoric of moments, they could not let their guard down.

Josh thought he would burst with happiness as Bronia led him to a nearby apartment where they could talk in private. Bronia was equally joyous but also distressed to find Josh suffering from whooping cough and measles and looking pale and gaunt. It was clear that he could not have survived much longer on his own. Going to a doctor was not an option but she could at least find him somewhere warm to rest and give him some hot fluids.

Josh recounted his time with the sisters, how he had run away and how he had survived the last few weeks alone on the streets. It was such a relief to have someone to talk to, someone who cared. He was also elated to be reunited with Rachel given the bond they had formed during their time in the bunker.

"What happened to Dad and Menasche?" Josh asked, his voice breaking.

Bronia's face darkened. "All I know is that they headed off to Katowitz to meet someone and disappeared," she replied, "I fear they were trapped and taken." They both knew that this meant transportation to Auschwitz. The news confirmed Josh's worst fears. Until that point, all he had known was that his father hadn't shown up for an arranged meeting. He had been desperately hoping for a less sinister explanation for his absence.

"As soon as I realised that they were missing, I knew we were at risk and had to move on from where we were staying," Bronia explained. "I didn't know where you were or how to find you. I could only hope and pray that you were safe," Bronia continued, not letting on to Josh that she had feared that he was lost too.

"What do we do now?" asked Josh quietly. Bronia pursed her lips, shook her head and hugged him. There was no easy answer to his question. But after the long, dark and lonely weeks they had endured, at least they now had each other.

As they talked into the night, Josh was filled with strong and conflicting emotions. There was the intense relief of being reunited with his mother and sister, the extreme sadness of knowing that his father and brother had been caught by the Nazis, and the ever-present fear that pervaded every waking moment. The capture of his father and brother highlighted the danger lurking around every corner.

Having found his mother and sister, Josh felt less alone but he had no pretensions that they were safe. They were still trapped in the belly of the beast, hoping beyond hope that, like the biblical Jonah, they would somehow be spat out onto dry land.

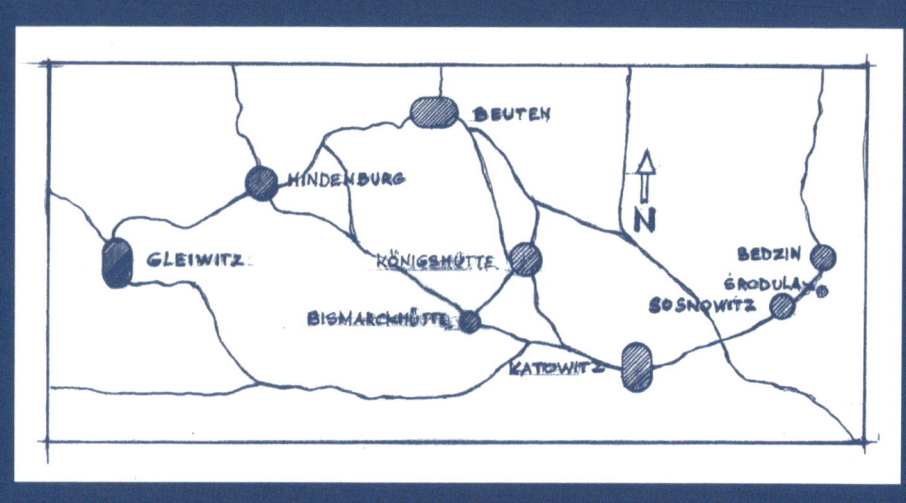

BRONIA, JOSH & RACHEL AVOIDED THE NAZIS BY MOVING CONSTANTLY THROUGH THE LOCAL TOWNS OF UPPER SILESIA. DRAWING BY JOSH PILA

38 ADDRESSES

A dark-haired woman in her late thirties came to the door of the apartment. "Can I interest you in some tobacco?" she asked. Josh and Bronia looked at each other, both sensing an opportunity in their relentless struggle for survival.

* * *

After running away from the dairy shop owner's network, Bronia maintained the cover story that Rachel, whom she referred to as 'Kusha', was a niece she was looking after while her father was on the Eastern front and her mother was ill in hospital. Bronia moved from town to town looking for house-cleaning jobs. Having cleaned someone's house, she would ask if she could stay the night rather than travel back to her home in a farming village.

Josh, whom she referred to as her nephew 'Hans', now accompanied Bronia as she moved around Silesia. They had a lot of repeat business and picked up new clients through word-of-mouth referrals. This effectively gave them a network of places to stay, which kept them off the streets. They later counted that they had slept at 38 different addresses over 11 months.

The small family was continuously on the move and always planning a few steps ahead—lining up their next cleaning job so that they had somewhere to go, and somewhere to spend the night. Their only belongings were a few spare clothes that they carried in a small bag. Rachel was not yet three years old and Bronia and Josh needed to look after her at all times, including providing her meals, finding her somewhere to sleep and watching over her. In addition to helping Bronia with the cleaning where he could, Josh supervised Rachel and did the shopping. They were paid in cash and food coupons which Josh would use to buy food. He had by now become very adept at the coupon system.

The family was still at constant risk. Their secret would be instantly exposed if anyone asked to see their identity papers. Further, they had to evade the suspicious eyes of the local *gauleiters*. As a day for attending church and spending time with family, Sundays were particularly difficult. In a deeply religious community, wandering around the streets on a Sunday would look conspicuous.

It was an exhausting and grinding existence.

* * *

One of the apartments that Bronia cleaned belonged to Mr Richlig. Mr Richlig was a bachelor in his forties with a medium build, a broad nose and thinning hair. He was generally quite friendly when sober, and, better still, he wasn't home much. He worked long hours in the steel works and would often go to the pub after work. His home was in a large block of apartments dedicated to workers at the nearby steel mill.

Bronia helped Mr Richlig with cleaning and cooking and was given a key to the apartment so that she could come in while he was working. It was Mr Richlig's apartment that Bronia took Josh to after their chance reunion.

Through the remaining months of the war, Mr Richlig's apartment became their fall-back destination when they had nowhere else to go. They stayed there overnight at least once a fortnight. It was the closest thing they had to a home. His apartment was very basic, it didn't even have its own toilet facilities. There was a communal toilet in the courtyard but going there involved potential exposure. It was safer to do their ablutions in pieces of newspaper and burn them in the fireplace.

They were cleaning Mr Richlig's apartment in March when a woman selling tobacco came to the door. While Bronia took some money out of her pocket to buy a small packet for Mr Richlig, both she and Josh saw an opportunity to significantly improve their chances of survival.

They spoke with the woman and ascertained that she lived with her family on a tobacco farm in Silesia. The family grew and cured the tobacco leaves before dividing them into 200-gram portions and wrapping them in paper for sale. Customers would then finely cut the smoked leaves and roll them in paper to form homemade cigarettes. In highly regulated occupied Poland, tobacco and cigarettes were only allowed to be purchased through an exchange of coupons. Selling tobacco door-to-door in this manner was illegal.

Bronia put a proposal to the woman. What if Bronia and Josh came to the farm on a regular basis to purchase the tobacco packages and they could do the door-to-door selling? For the woman, this was an attractive proposition and she immediately agreed. It meant that she could stay on the farm with her family rather than travelling around the towns. It also significantly reduced her risk of being arrested for making illegal sales.

The benefits for Bronia and Josh were enormous. It added to their cover story, giving them an additional plausible, if not legal, rationale for being out on the streets and moving from place to place. They could sell the tobacco for a mix of money and food coupons.

Access to coupons was critical, as money alone was not sufficient to buy basic food items, and they had no other way to legitimately obtain them.

Every few weeks, Bronia, Josh and Rachel would travel to the farm to pick up another batch of tobacco packages. They would bring the farmers supplies from town and would stay the night, often on a Sunday when it was highly suspicious to be out on the city streets. As the Russians continued their advance from the east, and the Nazis stepped up their efforts to exterminate the Jews, adding the tobacco-selling business to their survival kit almost certainly allowed the family to stay alive until the end of the war.

Josh relished the visits to the farm. The farmers were warm and welcoming and would let them join their family meals and sleep in the loft. They had three kids who Josh could play with; it was his only real opportunity to interact with children his own age.

Josh was, of course, measured about what he told his new friends but he enjoyed listening to their stories. They would sit under the fruit trees and observe the French prisoners of war who were assigned to work in the fields. "Look at those strange people. They go down to the river, catch frogs and then eat them!"

* * *

Sunday 30 April 1944 was a beautiful sunny day as Josh walked along the streets of Koenigshutte towards the main soccer stadium.

The walls of the buildings that lined the main street were covered in reminders that the war was still raging. Posters and signs warned the public to beware that their conversations may be overheard: '*Psst feind hort mit*—the enemy is listening." Advertisements on the walls and in the newspapers implored people to donate woollen gloves, hats, coats and blankets, alongside pictures of

German soldiers in the snow, freezing, suffering. Life for everyone under German occupation was becoming increasingly hard. Food was strictly limited and many products were simply not available. People had to make do with 'ersatz' (inferior substitute) products, such as chicory for coffee or apple peels to make tea.

But on that day, the war and all its hardships could be forgotten. There was a buzz around Koenigshutte, the excitement was palpable: Schalke 04 was in town.

Schalke 04 was the dominant club in the German soccer league between 1933 and 1945 and therefore featured heavily in Nazi propaganda. A match had been arranged between Schalke 04 and a representative team of players from various clubs in the Upper Silesian region. About 50,000 supporters flocked to the stadium from all over Upper Silesia, an enormous crowd for a 'friendly' soccer match in the middle of a war.

Josh had debated with his mother who had not wanted him to go. But he had seen the advertising for the game and could feel the build-up. He had not previously played or even watched a soccer game, but this was an exciting event and he didn't want to miss it. Yes, it was dangerous to be out amongst other people but, Josh argued, everyone's focus would be on the game. They would pay him no attention and he would be not out of place. As just another face in the crowd, Josh would be safer at the stadium than almost anywhere else.

Josh stood transfixed as he watched the game. For once he did not feel like an outsider, but at one with the rest of the crowd. His survival instinct was still on high alert—he made sure that at all times he had access to viable escape routes—but he relaxed as he watched the silky skills of the Schalke 04 players in their royal blue uniforms, as they prevailed eight goals to one.

For Josh, it was a rare respite from his daily struggle to survive. It was also the first chapter in his lifelong love of soccer.

* * *

Each night, Josh and Bronia discussed plans for the following few days, including where they would stay, particularly on the ever-problematic Sundays, and how to cash in their food coupons. They could get more per coupon for an ingredient, such as flour, than for a finished product, such as bread, but then they would need somewhere to bake their bread.

When making these plans, they acted collaboratively; their relationship was more like a partnership than parent and child. Josh had been first out of the ghetto and so had a head start on learning how to manage on the outside. It made sense for Josh to do jobs on the street, like purchase food, while Bronia cleaned and looked after Rachel. They became a working unit and even started thinking alike, rarely disagreeing on the best approach to get through their days.

They were always mindful not to behave in any way that would reveal their Jewish identity. Fortunately, they didn't look particularly Jewish, but, to be extra sure, Bronia put peroxide in Josh's hair to make it lighter, more Aryan. They even modified their diet to appear less Jewish, deliberately eating non-kosher food such as *'schpeck'*, pig fat that had been salted and smoked and could be spread on bread. Jews had long been accused of smelling of onion and garlic so Bronia and Josh made sure not to eat these foods.

Bronia told Josh about a form of code to covertly connect with another Jew. They would very quietly and surreptitiously say *"am choo*—your people" in Yiddish. To a non-Jew these words were not recognisable and would sound like someone clearing their throat. Bronia used this expression when she came across someone that she suspected of being Jewish, also hiding on the outside. It was comforting to talk openly to someone in the same predicament even when there was nothing they could do to help each other.

They were always on the move between Katowitz, Bismarckhutte, Koenigshutte, Beuten[20], Hindenburg[21] and Gleiwitz, all towns in the Upper Silesian region. These towns straddled the pre-1939 border between Germany and Poland, and had all been part of Germany before World War I. Their populations were more ethnically German than Polish. Bronia and Josh felt much safer in towns with a German than Polish demographic. Jews in Germany were generally more secular and assimilated than Jews in Poland where Jews made up a larger proportion of the population. Poles were considerably more likely to identify a Jew. Further, by this stage, the more Germanic towns had been clear of any Jewish presence for over four years—their Jewish populations had been relocated to towns such as Sosnowiec and Bedzin shortly after the war began. The local citizens did not expect to encounter any Jews and so tended to be less suspicious. To avoid being recognised, Bronia, Josh and Rachel avoided their hometown of Sosnowiec altogether.

Through cleaning and selling tobacco Bronia and Josh earned enough money and coupons to buy food. The small family was never in danger of starving. They always found somewhere to stay overnight and so were protected from the elements. The trio were, however, at all times in real and significant danger of being identified as Jews and sent to their deaths. They were constantly on edge, always on the look-out for the dangers that lurked in every corner. Even when asleep, their senses were highly tuned and they would be sensitive to every noise, however slight.

Their greatest exposure was their lack of official identity papers. It was practically unheard of for someone not to have the papers

---

20 During the occupation this town was known as Beuten but is now known by its Polish name, Bytom. 21 During the occupation this town was known as Hindenberg but is now known by its Polish name, Zabrze.

that established a person's right to live, work and spend coupons. At arbitrary times and in random places, people were asked by authority figures to show their papers. Bronia and Josh could improve their odds by avoiding places where people were more likely to be checked, such as near a police station. Still, it was immeasurably lucky that they were never caught without official documents.

Everything they did, every minute of every day, Bronia and Josh had to be aware of their surroundings and potential escape routes. If they went to a restaurant or a shop, they would always check for a second door they could escape through if danger came through the front door. Even on the street, they would look for alleys to run down or corners to hide behind. They relied heavily on their street smarts and gut instinct.

They were also attuned to people around them and what they might be thinking. Once in the town of Beuten, they were referred to a postal worker as a potential client for cleaning services. At the post office, they asked the woman at the counter to speak to that worker. The woman told them to wait there and not go away. Josh noted the look in the woman's eye and the way she told them not to leave. He sensed danger: the woman was suspicious and was going to turn them in. Josh tugged on Bronia's elbow and whispered that they needed to get out of there. They made a hasty retreat from the post office, jumped on the next tram and headed to another town.

*　*　*

The war in Europe raged on. On 6 June 1944, the Allies launched the second front, a massive invasion on the beaches of Normandy in France. With the Allies moving with great force from the west and the Russian army forcing the Germans to retreat in the east, it was becoming inevitable that Germany would lose the war.

On 20 July 1944, troops of the 1ˢᵗ Belorussian Front conducted a forced crossing of the Bug River and entered Poland.

On the same day, Hitler narrowly survived an assassination attempt. Conspirators from within the German high command sought to eliminate Hitler, seize control of the government and negotiate an end to the war on favourable terms. They detonated a bomb in a room where Hitler was conducting a war meeting. But for a series of unlucky events, Hitler's reign, the war and the Holocaust could have come to an abrupt end and countless Jewish lives would have been saved.

The Russian army lost precious time in its march across Poland. The Red Army reached the Vistula River on the outskirts of Warsaw in July 1944. Leaders of the Polish Home Army, nationalist resistance fighters, thought it was important to liberate their own country rather than waiting to be liberated by, and then falling under the regime of, Soviet communists. A widescale, but ultimately unsuccessful, revolt against the Nazi occupiers, known as the Warsaw Uprising, was launched by the Home Army. Under orders from Stalin, the Russian army waited on the sidelines while the intense street fighting continued, which delayed the eventual liberation of Warsaw and the rest of Poland by several months.

* * *

While the world around them was hostile and cold, Josh and Bronia were met, on occasion, with acts of kindness and warmth from unexpected sources. The woman who sold them tobacco fell in love with young Rachel, who had just turned three years old. She offered to look after the toddler while Bronia and Josh were on the road. Reluctantly, Bronia left Rachel with the woman in early October 1944, rationalising that Rachel would be much safer there. If disaster occurred and Josh and Bronia were caught, Rachel could at least have a life with the family on the farm.

This was the fate of many Jewish babies and toddlers. Left with non-Jewish families while their parents and siblings all perished, these young children grew up with no knowledge of their heritage. While it was a miracle that they survived, ultimately these children were lost to the Jewish community. After the war, Jewish agencies scoured European orphanages for lost children, fighting to 'reclaim' them for the Jewish faith.

It was also much easier and much less dangerous for Bronia and Josh to travel around without Rachel. They could move faster and did not have to worry about Rachel making a mistake that would inadvertently give them away. It was, in the circumstances, a good outcome for all concerned.

On Christmas Eve 1944, Josh and Bronia were working in Beuten at the apartment of a repeat client, an elegant, attractive lady in her mid-thirties. Realising that they had nowhere to go, she invited them to stay the night. As it turned out, that evening she was entertaining a senior German officer, a colonel in the Wehrmacht. When they realised the identity of the guest, Josh and Bronia became very nervous. They couldn't leave as it was already night and it would have been even more dangerous to be out on the streets on Christmas Eve. Instead, Josh and Bronia found themselves in the warm kitchen eating leftovers from the Christmas dinner: roast rabbit and vegetables and a special poppy-seed Christmas cake, crumbled and soaked in rum. It was the best meal they had eaten in years.

As they were eating, the lady opened the door to the kitchen and she and the German officer stepped in. "These are the people I was telling you about," she said, gesturing towards Bronia and Josh. The German, resplendent in his officer's uniform, had an amused smile on his face as he ran his eyes over Josh and Bronia, almost certainly realising that they were Jewish 'fugitives', particularly given they didn't have anywhere else to be for Christmas, but not inclined to take any action or turn them in. "Merry Christmas" was all that he said.

* * *

The Russian army continued its march west, and by the beginning of 1945, was headed towards Silesia. Believing their nightmare might soon be over, on 21 January 1945, Bronia and Josh picked Rachel up from the farm. It looked like they might survive.

Often during this period, Josh would tell Bronia that she was a heroine and that, if they were to survive, he would buy her a jewelled crown. They reflected on this often over future years. They agreed that Josh's children, Bronia's grandchildren, represented the crown and jewels that he had promised her.

LIBERATION

"*Ya Ivrai*—I am a Jew," Josh said to the Russian officer, using the few Russian words Bronia had taught him.

The officer, battle-hardened from years of fighting on the Eastern front, the most horrifying battlefield of World War II, stopped what he was doing, took a long hard look at Josh and started to cry. "*Kim mit mir*—Come with me" he replied to Josh in Yiddish.

Sunday 28 January 1945, a clear, crisp winter's day in Silesia. It was a good three months before the fall of Berlin and Germany's surrender, but for Josh it was the day the nightmare finally ended.

* * *

The Russian army was an unstoppable force as it rolled west across an enormous front, pushing the German army ever backwards towards the fatherland. The war had begun in Silesia, with the German invasion of Poland, and, by the end of January 1945, the Russians had pushed the Nazi invaders right back to the German border. However, the Russians had no intention of stopping there. Their target was Berlin and they were determined to get there before the Americans and British.

* * *

As Josh and Bronia devoured their unexpected Christmas feast in December 1944, the Third Reich was well and truly crumbling. It was suffering defeats from all sides inflicted by the Allied armies, and the German satellite states, including Romania, Bulgaria and Albania, were, one by one, overthrowing their governments and switching sides. Every German military professional knew that the war was lost, although Hitler still hoped for a fallout between Russia and the American/British governments that might halt their advance.

Warsaw was liberated on 17 January 1945, Krakow on 19 January 1945 and Auschwitz just a few days later on 27 January 1945.

As they waited for liberation, Josh and Bronia thought that the safest place for them was Mr Richlig's home in Bismarckhutte, so they returned there with Rachel for the last time.

Standing in a large grassy field across the road from the apartment, Josh watched Russian airplanes fly overhead. They flew so low that Josh could see the pilots in their cockpits and the Russian insignia on the wings. These were not large bombing planes but small reconnaissance aircraft, with just a single pilot. They were looking for any remaining German military presence in the town and would strafe military targets when they spotted them. Josh was not concerned about being hit by a stray bullet. In his mind, he was one of the 'good guys' and therefore at no risk of being hit by a Russian bullet.

On 26 and 27 January 1945, the German occupying forces left Bismarckhutte, which led to a temporary power vacuum and a breakdown of law and order. Gangs of drunken men roamed the town, looting shops and causing chaos.

Mr Richlig went out drinking on the evening of 27 January, joining the general mayhem in the streets. He did not arrive home until the next morning, very drunk on methylated spirits and highly agitated. It was the first time Josh had seen him in such a state.

"Who are you? Why aren't you at school?" Mr Richlig yelled at Josh as he pushed him around the room. He was an average-sized man but strong from working in the steel mill, while Josh was small and slight. He was no match for Mr Richlig and he was terrified as Bronia cowered to the side of the room, holding Rachel and pleading with Mr Richlig to stop.

In an alcohol-fuelled rage, Mr Richlig threw Josh against the standing oven in the middle of the apartment, hot from the coal that burned constantly through the winter, before opening the apartment window and threatening to throw Josh out onto the street two floors below.

As Mr Richlig's back was momentarily turned, Bronia grabbed their bag of belongings in one hand, and, with Rachel held in her other arm, she and Josh opened the door and raced out of the apartment. Mr Richlig yelled after them but did not give chase. They never saw him again.

* * *

The scene on the street was surreal. It was mid-morning and everything was white, covered in a thin layer of snow and ice. Most notable, however, was the quiet. After the mayhem and looting of the previous night, the streets were completely deserted, not a person or even a dog to be seen. It was as if a giant vacuum had sucked all life from the town.

Josh and Bronia knew that it was too dangerous to be outside and so headed down the main street towards the home of another previous client. As they walked, they saw three soldiers carrying rifles rounding the corner. The soldiers wore white overalls, white capes and had white material over their helmets.

Bronia was excited, thinking that they were Russian soldiers, and started moving towards them. Josh grabbed her elbow and pulled her back. "They're Germans," he whispered. Josh had read in the newspapers about special German units of commandos that wore white uniforms, rather than the standard green uniforms of the Wehrmacht, to camouflage themselves in the snow.

These were the last German soldiers to leave town, and they showed no interest in Josh, Bronia and Rachel even though it was highly suspicious that they were out on the street. After hiding their identity and surviving against all odds for so many months, Bronia and Josh had nearly exposed themselves in this final hour.

* * *

Josh and Bronia, still carrying Rachel, walked about a kilometre down the main road in the direction of Katowitz. They came to the apartment of the people they knew and knocked on the door. A middle-aged woman tentatively cracked open the door to look out. She was so flabbergasted to see who it was, she made the sign of the cross over her heart. She couldn't believe that they had been roaming the streets at this dangerous time.

The woman graciously invited them in and gave them soup and hot drinks. The apartment was small and sparse, but it was warm and the woman, who lived there with her 20-year-old daughter and baby granddaughter, was welcoming. A few short hours later the Russian army arrived.

* * *

Now a 10-year-old boy, but with his brother no longer beside him, Josh once again pressed his nose to the window and watched an invading army enter the town. Back in September 1939, despite the strength and power of the mighty Wehrmacht, all Josh had been able to see from his apartment window in Sosnowiec was a couple of soldiers wandering around the courtyard of his building. This time, from a second-floor window, he had a full and uninterrupted view of the strength and magnitude of an invading army as it marched into town.

First to appear down the street were three Russian soldiers, one on the right footpath, one on the left footpath and one walking down the middle of the road. These soldiers held their rifles and bayonets at the ready as they scanned the buildings on either side of the street for any sign of resistance. They had an unenviable role, to flush out signs of danger at great personal risk.

A tank rumbled down the road immediately after the three soldiers, ready to obliterate any house or building if a shot was fired from its window. No shots were fired, no resistance from the civilian population was evident.

More tanks followed, one after the other, for what seemed like hours. The tanks were followed by armoured vehicles, then trucks and infantry soldiers on foot. Those at the front were sharply dressed crack troops. However, the soldiers at the rear were increasingly bedraggled, troops from Russia's far flung provinces that had clearly received little or no training, were scrappily dressed and without modern firearms. At the very back of the infantry were Mongol soldiers wearing traditional pointed hats, which to Josh's eyes looked funny.

Finally, at the end of the parade, came horses and wagons carrying provisions. Tied to the wagons were livestock including cows, goats and sheep. It was standard protocol for the poorly resourced Russian armies to feed themselves. As they advanced across the countryside, they did not receive supplies from home as the American soldiers did, but instead would take what they needed from local farmers. This had a devastating effect on communities that were often left short of food after Russian soldiers swept through like a swarm of locusts.

The parade of military might continued all that day and the following two days. It was quite a spectacle, like the circus coming to town.

Josh was exhilarated as he watched the procession on the street below him. It felt like this army had come to save him, that he was a hero who had defied the might of the German army. They had tried to beat him but he had stared them down and come out on top. Now the Germans were running away as the Russian victory parade came to honour him. His chest burst with pride.

Late that afternoon, a truck pulled over to the side of the road and a Russian officer got out. The officer opened a map on the bonnet of the truck and studied it. Josh could not contain his excitement, and against his mother's wishes, he ran out onto the street. He walked up to the officer, a captain, stood as tall as he could, and proudly announced himself as a Jew, "*Ya Ivrai*," as if to say that he was the person they had come to see.

As it happened, the Russian officer was also Jewish. About 500,000 Jews served in the Red Army during World War II, many as officers due to their high standards of education. However, with some 30 million people serving in the Red Army during the war, it was still incredibly lucky that the officer Josh approached was also Jewish.

Having fought in the army as it had swept cross the Ukraine and Poland, this officer had seen the devastation of Jewish communities firsthand. Just the previous day, troops from General Konev's 1st Ukrainian Front (322nd Rifle Division, 60th Army) had liberated the Auschwitz concentration camp. The officer Josh approached would have heard about the industrialised murders that had occurred there and in other camps across Poland.

To find a Jewish child alive and well in Silesia, to have that child walk right up to him and announce himself, was beyond belief. A wave of emotion brought tears to the officer's eyes and left him momentarily lost for words.

"*Kim mit mir*—Come with me," he said to Josh in Yiddish. By responding in the German Jewish dialect spoken by Jews across Eastern Europe, the officer was not just using a common language, but he was creating an immediate and familiar bond.

In a way, this reaffirmed Josh's belief that the Russians had come to liberate people like him, that he was a hero, and would be treated like a king. This was, of course, far from reality. There was significant anti-Semitism within the Russian population and another officer would likely have given Josh a more hostile response. At the very least, he would have been shooed away, chastised for bothering an officer engaged in important military business. Again, lady luck intervened in Josh's favour.

Josh climbed into the truck with the Russian officer and they drove about a kilometre down the road, pulling up near the train station. The Russian officer was in charge of supplies and had received intelligence regarding a German food dump hidden in town. The officer had been searching for the site of this food dump when he had stopped his car to consult his map.

Near the train station there was a door and a set of stairs that took them far below the ground. Artificial lighting was required as they moved further and further out of the range of daylight. When they reached the bottom of the stairs, the officer opened a door, switched on the light and Josh gasped. After years of severe food restrictions, Josh saw before him a massive concrete cavern that stretched out under the railway line, as far as his eyes could see, stacked full of food. Josh saw enormous round cheeses—yellow and white—large barrels of sauerkraut and pickled cucumbers, and huge vats of butter. Josh could not believe his eyes; he felt that he was in wonderland. Clearly, the Germans, in their haste to leave, had not had time to take or destroy this incredible food store.

The Russian officer told Josh to choose whatever he wanted and arranged for a soldier and a car to take him home with his provisions. Josh was dropped on the sidewalk outside the building where he was staying with barrels of butter, sauerkraut, pickled cucumbers, sausages and cheeses. His new hosts and their neighbours had to help bring his bounty inside and wondered how he had come into possession of so much wonderful and precious produce. They were extremely happy that they had taken in Josh and his family and welcomed them to stay for as long as they needed.

Josh and Bronia regarded their liberation as a form of rebirth and for many years later they celebrated the anniversary of the arrival of the Russian army on 28 January.

RACHEL

After surviving the war, Rachel Pila passed away on 27 July 1945, her devoted mother and brother by her side. She was not yet four years old.

Rachel was born into a world that had gone mad. From the moment she was born she was a fugitive, targeted by the Nazi regime for the sole crime that she was Jewish. In her few short years, Rachel had been selected for deportation and murder during the *punkt*, spent extended periods hiding in a dark ghetto bunker, moved from house to house and town to town like a vagrant, and spent months separated from her family and living with strangers.

Rachel knew little joy in her short life: no fun, no laughter, no games, no childhood innocence. For the entirety of her existence her family lived with unrelenting stress, engaged every minute of every day in a life-or-death struggle. Food was limited, toys were non-existent. She never truly had a home.

* * *

The Nazis' hatred of the Jews had a strong racial basis. They viewed Jews as a parasitic, genetically inferior race that posed a clear danger to the 'superior' Germanic host nation. The Jewish threat had to be removed and this meant ridding society of Jewish blood entirely.

The genetic motives for the Nazi's policies explain why there was so much discussion and debate within the party as to who was defined as a Jew and what to do with 'half-Jews', people with mixed Jewish and non-Jewish blood. A converted Jew or a descendant of a mixed marriage, who had become a fully practising Christian, could still be subject to persecution if they had the requisite amount of Jewish ancestry.

It also explains why the Nazis targeted Jewish children. These children were not communists nor capitalists, had not stabbed anyone in the back and had played no part in Germany's defeat in World War I. The Nazi intent that they be eradicated was in no way rational, but rather was racist to the core.

Over one million Jewish children were murdered during the Holocaust. They were often the first to be killed, especially if they were too young to be used for forced labour. On arrival at the extermination camps, they were sent directly from the transports to the gas chambers.

* * *

Beautiful, dark-eyed Rachel could never have understood the sinister forces amassed against her. The evil ideology of Nazism, overlaying deeply entrenched anti-Semitism, meant she and her family were under unceasing threat all her life. Yet Rachel was wise beyond her years. With a maturity that belied her tender age, she knew instinctively that danger lurked all around. When hiding in the bunker in the ghetto, although less than two years old, she knew to keep perfectly quiet when they heard a warning signal from above. Moving around on the outside, she knew not to call Bronia 'mother', as this would conflict with their cover story.

She was never demanding in the way that young children usually are. She didn't cry or have tantrums. When Bronia and Josh were cleaning a client's home, Rachel always sat quietly and patiently in the corner.

RACHEL

Her parents fought valiantly for their beloved daughter. Bronia and Solomon felt guilty for bringing Rachel into the world in the middle of a firestorm, something they had not intended, and were determined to do everything they could to give her a chance at survival.

* * *

When Bronia and Josh collected Rachel from the farm in January, one week before their liberation, they were shocked at the state she was in. She had become very sick, had lost a lot of weight, and was pale and listless. She urgently needed to see a doctor but they could not take the risk and, in any event, medical attention was not readily accessible to civilians at that time. They had to wait for the Russian army to arrive and the Germans to leave before they could seek the medical attention Rachel so desperately needed.

From the apartment where they were staying in Bismarckhutte, they walked 10 kilometres to see a doctor in Katowitz, Bronia holding Rachel in her arms the whole way. The doctor told them that Rachel had contracted tuberculosis and that he would need to see her again to monitor her condition. It was quickly apparent that walking regularly to the doctor from Bismarckhutte was not viable and they would need to move to Katowitz.

Katowitz was the main city in the region and the headquarters for the regional Russian occupation force. Josh and his family registered themselves at the Russian headquarters and were assigned an apartment that had been vacated by an ethnic German family.

It was clear that the former occupants of the apartment had left in a hurry, dirty dishes still filled the kitchen sink. A substantial proportion of the Silesian population were of German origin and many ran away before the Red Army arrived, fearing they would be ill-treated by the Russians for collaborating with the Nazis.

Rachel had better access to medical attention once they were living in Katowitz, however, by this time there was little that the doctor could do for her. Had Silesia been liberated by the Americans, better medical treatment may have been available. Child survivors with tuberculosis in the West were commonly sent to a sanatorium in the Swiss Alps where the clean mountain air assisted in their recovery.

At one stage, on the doctor's recommendation, Rachel was admitted to a local hospital but she was very unhappy. Given there was not much the hospital could do to help Rachel, Bronia took her back to their home.

Over the next few months, Rachel's condition progressively deteriorated and Bronia rarely left her bedside, day or night. It was a tragically sad period for the family after all they had endured, particularly given that they had made it through to the point of salvation.

In July 1945, Rachel's brave fight ended and she succumbed to the disease that consumed her little body. By that time, the war in Europe was over, Germany lay in tatters and the Nazi regime was vanquished. Nevertheless, Rachel was murdered by the Nazis as surely as any other of the millions of Holocaust victims.

Adolf Hitler never met Rachel, he did not know her name or anything about her. Yet, it was the highest priority for him and his regime to murder her. In the midst of the largest war the world had ever known, and even once it became clear that the war was lost, Hitler devoted precious resources to killing Jews like Rachel. Despite the façade of the Nazi bureaucracy as an impersonal killing machine, it doesn't get much more personal than that.

Hitler died by his own hand in May 1945. Rachel stared the evil tyrant down and outlasted him.

* * *

Rachel was buried in the Jewish cemetery in Katowitz. Unlike the vast majority of child Holocaust victims who were buried in mass graves or reduced to ashes in crematoria, she was given a traditional Jewish burial attended by the remnants of her family: Josh, Bronia and Bronia's sister, Fela.

*JOSH, BRONIA, FELA & FELA'S NEW HUSBAND DAVID ZYCHER
AT RACHEL'S CONSECRATION*

JOSH SOLD NEWSPAPERS ON THE STEPS OF THE SILESIAN THEATRE, KATOWICE, 1945

REFUGEES & REUNIONS

In 1945 and 1946, Europe suffered a hangover the likes of which had never been seen. People, families, communities and countries were broken, destitute and lost. The continent was awash with refugees, a sea of humanity that had been cut loose and cast adrift, searching for solid ground on which to rebuild their lives.

It was in Poland that the war had begun in 1939, when the country had been overrun by the blitzkrieg *tactics of the German army. After years of oppressive occupation, the Poles were finally liberated by the Russian army as it swept towards Berlin.*

At its essence, the Eastern European theatre of World War II was a battle between the two great European land powers of the day, Germany and Russia, over the European heartland. The buffer states that lay between them—Poland, Ukraine, Belarus—were the stomping grounds on which this great power struggle played out. The toll on civilians in these regions was horrendous.

After being almost extinguished, an ember of Jewish presence flickered back to life in towns and cities across Poland. The few survivors from the extermination camps and the death marches started to trickle back to their home towns. Polish Jews who had escaped to Russia early in the war returned. Jews hiding in bunkers emerged and many Jewish children entrusted to orphanages or friendly neighbours shed their Christian identities. All began the desperate search for surviving family and friends.

While Bronia had been dedicated to caring for Rachel, Josh, at the tender age of 10, became the primary breadwinner for the family. With no school to attend, Josh could fully dedicate his time to generating income. Each morning, he would buy a large batch of newspapers. He would then position himself at the top of the six steps leading up to the Silesian Theatre[22] which looked out onto the market square and its criss-crossing tram tracks. The area teemed with people, hurrying to work or to the market, and Josh would sell his papers quickly.

In addition to the small profit made on the sale of each paper, these transactions served another important purpose. The currency used in Silesia during the German occupation was the reichsmark. Since the region had been liberated and back under the control of the Polish government, the economy was shifting back to the use of the Polish currency, zloty. Reichsmarks could be converted to zlotys but only for a limited time and only in small amounts. Any leftover reichsmarks would be worthless. Cleverly, Josh was using his newspaper business to enact unofficial currency conversions. He bought the newspapers with reichsmarks and sold them for zlotys.

Once the papers for the day were sold, Josh moved on to his other businesses. Bronia learnt to make soap at home that Josh could sell at the market. They also purchased lollies—such as candy sticks and coloured fish made from sugar—from a manufacturer in one-kilogram boxes, repackaged them into smaller boxes and sold them for a profit.

Josh and Bronia lived in an apartment on the third floor of a building at 9 Piastowska Street, a short road just a few streets away from the Silesian Theatre. It was a box-shaped building, with big square windows, built in the 1920s. A field behind their apartment block turned into an unofficial marketplace each day. People would gather and sell, often by way of barter, anything they didn't immediately need. It was almost impossible to purchase new goods, so if, for

---

[22] The Silesian Theatre is the largest theatre in Silesia, built in the early 1900s and dedicated to Stanisław Wyspianski, the famous Polish playwright, painter and poet.

example, someone needed shoes, their only option would be to seek out someone with a spare pair of shoes and trade with them.

It was at this market that Josh sold his soap and lollies, displaying his stock in a tray at his waist supported by a strap around his neck. When he had emptied his tray, he could quickly go back to the apartment for more supplies.

* * *

Within weeks of liberation, the Red Cross set up soup kitchens, usually near railway stations. The homeless and displaced were served steaming bowls of soup together with a slice of bread from big vats warmed over large stoves. No seating was provided, patrons would eat standing up.

Apart from providing much-needed warm meals, these sites served as meeting places for lost souls. Alongside each soup kitchen was a Red Cross office where rudimentary records were kept. These provided a first port of call for survivors looking for lost relatives.

In the coming months, Jewish organisations set up more sophisticated information exchanges, where survivors could register their names, search for information about family members and leave notes in the desperate hope that their messages might be picked up by loved ones.

The Jewish community centres became the primary communication amongst refugees who had no phones and no fixed addresses. They were the venues for emotional reunions and for the exchange of news, sometimes exhilarating but often devastating. A visitor could be elated to hear that a family member had been seen alive but far too often the news was soul-crushing confirmation of their loved one's murder at the hands of the Nazis.

Bronia and Josh desperately sought out anyone who could shed light on the fate of Solomon and Menasche. They spoke to several Auschwitz survivors who all told them the same story.

Solomon and Menasche had arrived at Auschwitz and Menasche, aged just 12 years old, had been sent immediately to the gas chambers. Solomon was devastated. His eldest son had been murdered and he had no idea of the fate of his wife and other two children. He did not believe they had any chance of surviving.

In deep despair, Solomon attempted to take his own life by slitting his wrists but the authorities in Auschwitz stopped him. Instead he was assigned to the *sonderkommandos*, one of the worst work units in the camp. These unfortunate souls were responsible for removing the dead bodies from the gas chambers and taking them to the ovens for cremation. Because they witnessed Germany's most extreme crimes, the Nazis had a policy of killing off the contingent of *sonderkommandos* every few months and replacing them with a new contingent. It is likely that Solomon was killed after several months of working in this horrendous role.

* * *

Shortly after the war began, many Jews realised that they were in danger of losing their valuables. If they took them with them when they were deported to the labour camps or concentration camps, they would be stolen by the Germans. The Nazis collected enormous amounts of valuables from their victims—jewellery, watches, clothes and even gold teeth—and transported them to Germany. When Jews were deported to the ghettoes, their homes were occupied by Poles or relocated Germans. Any valuables left in their homes fell into the hands of the new occupants.

The only way Jews could preserve their valuables was to hide them. Small, highly valuable items, like jewellery, could be hidden in secret compartments in furniture or buried in the garden, in the hope that one day they would return and recover them.

In some cases, Jews imprisoned in concentration camps would use their hidden treasure to bribe a guard for additional food, or some other assistance. They would direct the guard to the treasure, buried in a garden or hidden in a secret location.

In most cases, the Jews did not return, and the valuables were lost forever, like hidden pirate treasure with no treasure map.

* * *

Early in the German occupation, Solomon bought two tins of flint stones to hide in the garden, hoping to retrieve them once the war was over. He regarded flints as commodities that, unlike cash, would always hold their value. He put the two tins into a larger tin, which he then buried in the garden immediately behind the apartment block on Sienkewicza Street. He showed Bronia where they were hidden.

After liberation, Bronia remembered the flints and knew that they would be valuable at a time when Josh and Bronia were struggling to earn money. However, she was too frightened to go back to Sosnowiec to look for them. Many returning Jews had been severely beaten or killed by the Poles who had taken over their houses and belongings and did not want to relinquish them.

At the Jewish community centre in Katowitz, Bronia came across a second cousin on the Pila side who was an officer in the Polish division of the Russian army. She asked him to accompany her and Josh to Sosnowiec to look for the flints; she felt much safer escorted by a man in military uniform.

The three of them took the tram to Sosnowiec and made their way to 1 Sienkewicza Street. As they entered the courtyard, Josh noted that it looked just as they had left it four years earlier. They did not see who was currently occupying their apartment and made no attempt to recover any other belongings. They simply went around the back of the apartment, dug up the large tin, with the two smaller tins of flints inside, filled in the hole and left without looking back. This was no longer their home.

Outrageously, the relative took one of the tins of flints as payment for escorting them on this recovery mission. This left Josh and Bronia with the other tin of flints. At that time, it was by far the most valuable thing that they owned. Josh sold a few of the flints in the market. Compared to the soaps and lollies that he had been peddling, the flints were much more profitable.

To protect them from being stolen, Bronia hid the remainder of the flints in a box of lollies. A few weeks later, she accidentally sold that box of lollies, forgetting that the flints were inside. Their treasure was lost. It was a rare mistake by Bronia, fortunately one that cost them only money, and not their lives.

* * *

The Nazis had descended on Poland and its Jews like a tidal wave, smashing and drowning everything in its path. Jewish communities were washed away, like sandcastles when the tide comes in, as if they had never been there.

As the tide receded, the flotsam and jetsam of broken lives was left behind. Disoriented Jews started to surface, dazed and traumatised, almost surprised to find themselves alive. They had survived. They knew that the chances of finding family members alive was slim, yet they had to look. What else was there to do?

* * *

One day in Katowitz, Bronia bumped into a woman she had known before the war. The woman told Bronia that her sister, Fela, was alive and staying in Bedzin. Fela had survived Auschwitz but her son and ex-husband had been killed. She had not come with the woman to look for survivors in Sosnowiec or Katowitz because she assumed the rest of her family had all died.

Bronia couldn't go to Bedzin because, at that time, she was preoccupied with looking after Rachel. She implored the woman to pass on a message to Fela to let her know she was alive. At the first available opportunity, her sister came to Katowitz to see Bronia. The reunion was both joyous and tearful. Against all odds, the sisters were reunited. They had both lost so much but at least had each other.

Bronia had another sister, Regina, who had been married to a man called Joseph Levit. Regina, Joseph and their children, were murdered in the war. Isaac Levit, Joseph's younger brother, and two of his sisters had been liberated from the Buchenwald concentration camp in Germany by the United States army. Isaac got papers allowing him to travel back to Poland to search for surviving family members. Isaac was very pleased to find Bronia, his brother's sister-in-law.

Karl Pila was Solomon's youngest brother. He was only 17 when the war began and still living with his parents. He was in the Srodula ghetto and captured during the major actions in August 1943 and deported to Auschwitz, where he miraculously managed to survive. When the Nazis evacuated the extermination camp, the inmates were forced to march west back to Germany. There he was liberated from a camp by the Americans.

Karl also obtained official US government papers permitting him to return to Poland to search for relatives. When he came to Sosnowiec he heard on the grapevine that Bronia and Josh were in Katowitz. When he found them, he told them that two of his other brothers, Usher and Victor, had also survived, but tragically both had lost their wives and children. The three brothers were all living in Munich.

Over the next year, Karl made several visits to Poland under his specially sanctioned visa. This was not solely for family reunification reasons. He also used his papers to smuggle truckloads of American cigarettes into Poland, which he then sold at enormous profits.

OPERATION BRICHA

*'From Stettin in the Baltic to Trieste in the Adriatic,
an iron curtain has descended across the continent.'*

WINSTON CHURCHILL, 5 MARCH 1946, FULTON, USA

* * *

On 1 January 1945, the Provisional Government of the Republic of Poland was established. It was largely comprised of Polish communists with close ties to the communist party of the Soviet Union.

The following month, US president Franklin D. Roosevelt, British prime minister Winston Churchill and Soviet premier Joseph Stalin met in Yalta, a town in the Crimea, to discuss the progress of the war and the organisation of the post-war world. The three world leaders agreed that democracies would be established and free elections would be held in all liberated European countries, including Poland.

However, Poland in fact remained under Soviet control and a number of Polish politicians who opposed the communist party were arrested and subjected to show trials. For the next 40 or so years, Poland was subject to authoritarian governments and its people were denied the liberties and freedoms enjoyed by those who lived in countries on the other side of the Iron Curtain.

Life in post-war Poland was particularly difficult for the Jews whose families, communities and businesses had been destroyed.

POALE ZION MEETING WITH YA'AKOV ZERUBAVEL, A FAMOUS ZIONIST ACTIVIST (BEARDED MAN, MIDDLE). JOSH (MIDDLE ROW, FAR RIGHT) WOULD BE THE ONLY CHILD AT THESE MEETINGS, KATOWICE, 1946

Anti-Semitism continued to run rampant among the Poles, who did not want to return property taken from the Jews during the Nazi occupation, or who blamed the Jews for the communist regime that had been imposed on them.

Crime and violence against Jews, prevalent throughout Poland, culminated in a vicious pogrom in the town of Kielce in July 1946. Jews were wrongly accused of kidnapping a young boy, resulting in an outbreak of hostilities that resulted in more than 40 Jews killed and a similar number injured.

Ninety percent of the 3.3 million Jews who had lived in Poland prior to the war had been murdered. Those returning after the war found their families slaughtered, communities decimated and synagogues destroyed. Most realised that Poland was not the place for them to rebuild their lives. Of the more than 250,000 Jews in Poland after the war (about 50,000 had survived in Poland, the others had returned from the east), 150,000 left between 1945 and 1948, most of them illegally.

* * *

Like most Jewish survivors in Poland, Josh and Bronia desperately wanted to leave. With their home presumably occupied and family murdered, there was nothing left for them there but bad memories. Initially, at least, they wanted to get to Munich where Isaac Levit and three of Solomon's brothers were living.

They joined Poale Zion (Workers of Zion), one of the many socialist Zionist movements that formed in the post-war period. As was the case before the war, political associations proliferated across the Jewish community. Most were Zionist movements representing various shades of socialist ideologies. The Bundist organisation, which did not support the establishment of a separate Jewish state, had fallen out of favour following the devastation of the Holocaust. The need for a Jewish homeland as a place of refuge was evident to all.

The Poale Zion movement created 'kibbutzim' in Katowitz. Groups of survivors lived together in flats, and shared everything they owned, much like in the kibbutzim in Palestine. These Polish kibbutzniks taught themselves about agriculture and talked about getting to Palestine and working the land.

Josh and Bronia did not live in a Katowitz kibbutz but they did attend regular meetings with other members of Poale Zion. The meetings were mainly social, an opportunity to congregate to exchange information and discuss rumours. People brought baked cakes, usually butter cake with *streusel*.

Josh would be the only child at these meetings; Bronia was not prepared to leave him at home alone. In the first few months after the war, there were very few child survivors his age.[23] The others at the meetings were in disbelief that he was there and, often having lost their own children, treated Josh like a living miracle. He felt very special.

Sometimes, an emissary from the Yishuv, the Jewish settlement in Palestine, would come to the meetings and talk about developments there, British attempts to block Jewish immigration, and the various ways Jews were managing to immigrate illegally. The most distinguished of these emissaries was Ya'akov Zerubavel, a highly influential Zionist figure and one of the leaders of the Poale Zion movement. At a meeting attended by Zerubavel, Josh recited a poem in Polish that he had written, lamenting the mean-heartedness of the British in not allowing people who had suffered so much to enter the land where they could finally feel safe. In this poem, Josh let his anger and frustrations spill out.[24]

At first, Bronia and Josh attempted the legal route to emigrate. They travelled by train to Warsaw to visit government offices and apply for passports and travel visas allowing them to leave

---

23 Several months after the liberation of Poland, Jewish families started returning from Russia so Jewish children Josh's age became less of a rarity. 24 Poetry as a genre very much resonated with Josh. He loved studying the works of the great poets in school and could quote their words decades later.

Poland. En route, they saw the destruction inflicted on the city of Warsaw. Around 80 percent of the buildings were bombed out. The combined impacts of the German invasion of 1939, the quashing of the Warsaw Ghetto uprising in 1943 and the Home Army's uprising of 1944, had left the city flattened. Trams ran between the piles of rubble. With limited manpower and resources, restoration of the city would take decades.

Josh and Bronia's request in Warsaw for passports and visas was declined. Refusing to be deterred, they began to plan their illegal escape.

* * *

'Bricha', the Hebrew word for 'flight' or 'escape', was the name given to a clandestine operation to smuggle Jews out of Eastern Europe into Allied-occupied Western Europe, and from there, on to Palestine. It was conceived by Jewish members of the Polish resistance who joined forces with the Jewish Brigade, a unit of the British army comprised of Jewish soldiers from Palestine, and the Haganah, a Jewish paramilitary organisation in Palestine.

Jews were smuggled out of Poland by train, around 200 people at a time. They were taken across the Polish borders with Czechoslovakia and Hungary and into displaced persons (DP) camps in Germany, Austria and Italy. A network of stopovers was established along the way. US zone commanders and Czech border officials unofficially permitted the infiltration of these illegal refugees.

Around 150,000 Jews were relocated through Operation Bricha. Approximately 50,000 between August 1945 and June 1946, and another 100,000 in the months following the Kielce pogrom of July 1946.

* * *

Back in Katowitz, Josh and Bronia let it be known that they wanted to join Operation Bricha and were allocated to an expedition that was to leave Sosnowiec in September 1946. The exact timing of the departure was uncertain so they had to be ready to leave at short notice. They packed their few belongings and went to stay with Fela. At this stage, Fela was living in Sosnowiec with her new husband, who had started a business manufacturing quilts.

From Sosnowiec they travelled to Waldenburg[25], a town in Lower Silesia very close to the Czechoslovakian border. This was the final staging point and the organisers needed to wait until the conditions were right to make the escape. Josh was not privy to these conditions but presumably they were waiting for the guards they had bribed to be rostered on to the border crossing.

In Waldenburg they were put up in apartments and they undertook training drills in promptly following instructions. They practised getting the group of 200 men, women and children on and off the train in a matter of minutes. The group was told to be ready to leave at any time, day or night, with no more than five minutes' notice.

Finally, the fateful night arrived. The message was passed around that they were to leave immediately. Josh was brimming with excitement and anticipation. He had been eager to get out of Poland for a long time.

Bronia and Josh each carried a small suitcase containing their worldly belongings. In addition to his clothes, hidden in a false bottom of Josh's wooden suitcase, was their treasure: a couple of gold US coins, an antique Austro-Hungarian coin and a British five pound note. They had purchased these items with their remaining Polish currency as they were portable and would presumably have value in the West. The five pound note was larger than an A4 sheet and had to be folded multiple times. Much later they discovered that the note was a forgery. The Nazi regime had printed large quantities,

---

25 Polish name Walbrzych.

potentially hundreds of millions of pounds, of fake British currency with the intent of damaging the British economy.

With these treasures hidden in his suitcase, Josh guarded it closely. He sat on his case during waking hours and used it as a pillow when he slept.

The train used for this operation was a cargo train, with big red wagons that opened with sliding doors and no steps. Eerily similar to the cattle trains used to deport Jews to the extermination camps, this one would take them to freedom.

The Nazi trains had been massively overcrowded, with no concern for the comfort or amenity of the passengers. The Nazis didn't care whether their passengers survived the trip. The Operation Bricha trains were quite different. Although they were very basic with no lights, beds or dining cars, passengers could sit or lie down on the floors, and they had regular stops to stretch their legs, have something to eat, or use the bathroom.

The first border crossing, into Czechoslovakia, was the most dangerous as it was guarded by Russian soldiers, who were more motivated to enforce rules. The passengers sat in the train for hours, not moving, just inside the border. They were told to remain silent so as not to reveal that the train was full of people. At one stage, all 200 of them had to get off the train and then get back on again. No-one told them why. The passengers had to rely on the organisers and trust that they knew what they were doing.

Trusting others was a stark contrast to the strategy Josh and Bronia had used to survive the final months of the war, when they could trust no-one but themselves. However, by now, Josh felt quite relaxed about relying on others to make decisions. The stakes were nowhere near as high. If caught, they would have been sent back to Poland, not killed.

The refugees went to sleep on the train and awoke the next morning in Czechoslovakia, near the town of Brno. All breathed a huge sigh of relief. The biggest hurdle had been traversed; the trip would be a success.

The train travelled through Czechoslovakia for four or five days before approaching the Austrian border. The Austrian border guards were welcoming and the Czech border guards were obviously not overly concerned about people smuggling. They were prepared to look the other way while the train crossed the river into Austria in broad daylight.

The train stopped in Vienna, about half an hour from the border. The organisers told the passengers the journey would be easier from this point as they were no longer in a country controlled by the Soviet Union.

In Vienna, they spent a few days at a makeshift halfway house for Jewish refugees. It was the old Rothschild Hospital, named after its founder Baron Anselm von Rothschild and opened in 1873 as a hospital for the local Jewish community. It had been closed by the Nazis in 1943 but reopened after the war to serve as a hospital for sick and infirm displaced persons. From 1945 to 1952, the Rothschild Hospital provided shelter for 250,000 Jewish refugees on their way to a new life. It was a beautiful, grand building but overcrowded with the huge number of refugees. Josh and Bronia explored the building looking for somewhere to spend the night but ultimately found themselves sleeping for two nights on the grand staircase.

Josh had a sense of comfort being surrounded by so many Jewish refugees, he felt that there was safety in numbers. Compared to the days where he had to be obsessively careful about every detail of what he did and what he said, he was relatively carefree. His only concern was to guard his few possessions.

The next stop on their journey was Linz, where they spent a few days before travelling on to Salzburg. In Salzburg, they were put up in a Jewish DP camp for about two weeks. The camp was reasonably full but not overcrowded. It felt like a luxury to spread out and sleep in single beds in the large barracks.

Each person also received meals and some pocket money in Austrian schillings. The meals were typical Austrian food: bread, herrings, potatoes, sauerkraut, sausages and meat patties. All appealed to Josh's continental taste buds and remained amongst his favourite foods throughout his life.

The camp was surrounded by a fence and some guards. Josh didn't feel that these were designed to keep people in but rather to protect them from people outside, people who might still have ill feelings towards Jews or who might want to steal their belongings and food. However, he had an overwhelming urge not to be confined; he loved to roam and hated to be hemmed in. While Josh could have requested permission to leave the camp through the front gates, he preferred to sneak out. He had recent experiences of escaping through fences and avoiding guards. He went in and out of the DP camp at least twice a day and wandered the streets of Salzburg, using the small amount of pocket money to purchase goods, usually food items, that he thought his mother might like. It was a bonus that products were cheaper on the outside than at the camp canteen. He felt independent, free and empowered.

Interaction with other refugees in the camp was limited. Although Josh was proficient in Yiddish, German, Polish, and to a lesser extent, Russian, people kept to themselves and were not inclined to talk about their experiences during the war. In any event, there were very few children for Josh to interact with.

Finally, Josh, Bronia and their travelling companions were told that it was time to leave for the last part of their journey. They again boarded the goods train and crossed the border into Germany. They were deposited in a DP camp in Landshut, about 30 kilometres outside of Munich.

It was a cold and wet day and to Josh the camp looked miserable. Refugees cowered in tents trying to stay warm, the fields were covered in mud. Josh took one look and said to Bronia, "We know people in Munich, we don't have to stay here."

Josh went back to the train station and jumped on a goods train to the Munich central station. He then walked to 3 Holzstrasse, the address he had been given for Isaac Levit who lived with his younger sister Helen and her husband David Hertzberg.

To Josh, Munich felt very foreign. Although, by this stage, Josh spoke fluent German, when he asked a train conductor for directions to Holzstrasse, he could not understand the conductor's strong Bavarian accent, and had to ask for the directions to be repeated three times.

Finally, Josh arrived at David Hertzberg's apartment unannounced. David and Isaac knew that Josh and Bronia were hoping to move to Munich but they had no idea when or how. As he had done to his father and brother all those months back in Srodula, Josh appeared out of the blue, like an apparition.

When Josh knocked on the door and introduced himself, David greeted him with a mix of excitement and surprise and warmly welcomed him inside. "We just arrived. Mum is waiting at the DP camp," Josh told David. As soon as Isaac arrived home, they headed back to the camp to collect Bronia.

MUNICH

Munich was the birthplace and ideological epicentre of the Nazi party. The Nazis themselves referred to the city as '*Hauptstadt der Bewegung*—Capital of the Movement'. As such, it was an unlikely location for the metaphoric rebirth of a young Polish Jewish boy.

Since liberation, Josh had lived in Katowitz for a year and half, free from the fear of extermination. However, during that time, he and Bronia had barely kept afloat, looking after Rachel and trying to earn enough money to survive. It was not the typical life of a pre-teen boy.

In post-war Munich, Josh was able to reclaim his childhood, and live a life of relative normality full of school, soccer practise, friends, family, fun and light-hearted experiences. For the first time since he was five years old, Josh could focus on living and not merely surviving.

Europe was still in turmoil, but for Josh it was a wondrous time.

* * *

The defeat of Germany at the end of World War II was total and devastating. Germany lost its sovereignty and was partitioned into four zones, administered by the Soviet Union, the United States, England and France. Munich was the headquarters of the American zone.

IN MUNICH, JOSH (FRONT ROW, MIDDLE) JOINED THE SCHOOL SOCCER TEAM AND BEGAN TO RECLAIM HIS CHILDHOOD

Conditions were tough in Munich. About 60 percent of the city buildings had been reduced to rubble during the war. This caused severe housing shortages, exacerbated by the arrival of millions of ethnic Germans who were forcibly evicted or chose to run away from Poland, Czechoslovakia, Hungary and the Baltic states.

Germany's economic infrastructure had largely ceased to function. Many senior business leaders had been members of the Nazi party and were now being hunted by the authorities. Inflation was rampant and the currency was frequently devalued.

To make matters worse, there were significant food shortages. Much of Germany's agriculture was in the Soviet zone and the Soviets were more intent on exacting reparations for losses suffered during the war than on feeding the population of western Germany. Providing food for Germany became a major expense for the taxpayers of the United States and Britain.

* * *

In 1946, the Jewish population of the western zones of Germany numbered about 75,000. In Munich there were several thousand Jews, mostly Eastern European survivors. Many had escaped from the death marches out of the Polish and German extermination camps. Others, like Josh and Bronia, had emigrated from the east, mostly illegally.

As Jews have done throughout their history, they quickly banded together to form communities, to support and protect each other, and to foster their religious and cultural life.

Josh and Bronia stepped into this world in the autumn of 1946. Connecting with family members provided a link to the past but in all other respects they were ready to establish a new life. For them, it was a form of rebirth, a fresh start.

The past was filled with tortured ghosts and nightmares, despair and fear. They had lost so much, everything except each other.

The currents of history had washed them up on new shores, anchorless and displaced, battered and exhausted. They needed to establish roots on which they could build their futures.

In Munich, Josh finally felt safe after so many years as a fugitive having to conceal his identity. He no longer needed to hide in the shadows or be frightened of strangers. In fact, he felt victorious, like a conqueror. He had stared down the Nazis and won his personal war. He could hold his head high and feel strong and secure. No-one could take that triumph and power away from him.

When Bronia and Isaac Levit struck up a romance and then married in February 1947, it was a further break from the past and a shift in focus to the future. Determined to rebuild their lives, they formed a new family unit.

Weddings such as Bronia and Isaac's, in the immediate aftermath of the war, had many of the typical trimmings of Jewish weddings: two adult witnesses, the bride and groom standing under the *chupah*, the breaking of the glass. However, these weddings often differed from typical Jewish weddings in one important respect—there was no rabbi. After the murder of so many Jews, there were simply not enough rabbis available to officiate, so a friend or an acquaintance who knew the relevant prayers would conduct the ceremony.

Bronia and Isaac were married at a friend's home. It was a small celebration attended by their few remaining family members and a small number of friends. Josh was pleased to see Bronia beaming happily, but he couldn't help feeling uneasy.

Josh liked Isaac; he was a decent, principled man who cared greatly for Bronia. But there was no definitive confirmation that his father was dead, and in his heart, Josh still dreamed that one day Solomon would be found. Maybe, somehow, he had survived Auschwitz as several of his brothers had. Could he be stuck behind the Iron

Curtain, unable to get to them, or was he disoriented and lost? Josh never lost hope that his father would someday return... not until so many years had passed that it seemed impossible that he could still be alive.

While Isaac became Josh's stepfather, he did not take on a significant parental role. Isaac was sensitive to the fact that Josh was already 12 years old and highly independent. If Isaac did have any parental views in relation to Josh, he would pass these through Bronia and never take them up with Josh directly.

One of the few parental activities that Isaac shared with Josh was their regular outing to watch professional wrestling. The wrestling was held in a nearby building which housed a permanent circus. Josh relished these outings and learnt the names of the different wrestlers and their strengths and weaknesses.

* * *

When they had first arrived in Munich, Josh and Bronia stayed for a short while with the Hertzbergs in Holzstrasse. They were generous and welcoming. David Hertzberg was highly industrious. He had a fledgling, though not entirely legal, business bottling brandy in the apartment in which they all lived. Josh was given the job of putting on the labels.

David's younger brother, Shmuel, also lived with them. He was taller, darker and more handsome than his brother, but far less industrious. He was a happy-go-lucky type who was primarily focused on meeting girls. David, Helen and Shmuel ultimately moved to the United States. Their priorities in Munich provided a window into their future prospects: David became a successful property developer, while Shmuel drove a taxi in New York.

With enormous numbers of displaced persons, both Jewish and non-Jewish, still languishing in DP camps many months after the end of the war, the American administrators decreed that local Germans had to accommodate the refugees. The housing ministry assessed buildings and apartments, considered who was living there and how many people they could take in. Jews were given priority.

Josh and Bronia were initially assigned to share a small, two-bedroom apartment with a German lady. It was on the first floor of an apartment block and in good condition. Josh and Bronia had one bedroom and the local lady had the other bedroom. They shared the kitchen and lounge room. The local lady was very quiet and kept to herself. Though she never complained, it was clearly an imposition for her to have these foreigners in her home and their interactions were somewhat awkward.

When Bronia and Isaac got married, the family moved into a four-bedroom apartment shared with a German family comprising a mother, two daughters in their twenties, and a boy named Gunter who was just one year older than Josh. The older of the daughters had a permanent boyfriend who also lived with them. The younger daughter had lots of suitors in the US army. Gunter was tall and blond and Josh liked playing soccer with him in the street. The household was crowded and busy, but everyone got on well.

* * *

She'erit Hapletah literally means 'the leftovers of the remnants'. It was the name given to a database of Holocaust survivors compiled in 1946 and has become a term to describe the Jews left standing when the tide of Nazi hate receded from German-occupied Europe.

It was also the name appearing on an illuminated sign, in both Hebrew and Latin letters, above a Jewish restaurant opened in Munich in 1947 by Bronia and Isaac, in partnership with another couple. The restaurant, located in an old German pub, offered traditional Jewish/Polish dishes: chicken soup, lochshen, gefilte fish and potato latkes. The food was delicious.

Bronia and Isaac were equal parts excited and nervous about their new business venture. Neither had prior restaurant experience but they were ready to put in the hard work necessary to succeed.

The chef was a non-Jewish Greek man who specialised in cakes. The waiters were all German, very professional and experienced. Bronia and the female partner supervised the kitchen, while Isaac and the male partner sourced the ingredients. They would drive out to the countryside to buy specialist livestock, such as geese and ducks. For this purpose, Isaac bought a car, a large, gunmetal grey, convertible Mercedes, with sideboards on both sides and a big bonnet with vents. They were told that it had previously been owned by Adolf Hitler; it was his Munich car! The bittersweet irony that it was now being driven by Jews to source food for a Jewish restaurant in the heart of Munich was not lost on anyone.

Josh was not directly involved in the decision making around the restaurant. He was no longer Bronia's partner-in-survival and their relationship had reverted to the more traditional mother-and-son roles. Josh was more than content with this outcome. He went to the restaurant every day after school and would eat his dinner on his own at a table near the kitchen. The restaurant had an orchestra and a dance floor. The drummer taught him how to play the drums and some evenings Josh would be given a cameo role performing with the orchestra.

Josh loved spending time at the restaurant. When not playing the drums, he amused himself by observing the patrons, an eclectic and colourful group. The Jewish survivors had all endured unimaginable horrors and were now determined to live it up. The restaurant was also popular amongst Jewish American soldiers, people from another world, but who shared cultural traits, including the love of traditional Jewish fare.

In November 1946, at the age of 12, Josh attended school for the first time. It was a small Jewish school in an old mansion on Moehlstrasse, across the road from the Jewish Community Centre.

The co-educational school was a melting pot of Eastern European Jewish survivors. The teachers were predominantly Lithuanian and Latvian and were first-rate educators. The kids came mostly from Russia, including Polish children who had spent the war in Russia, but also included children from Romania, Lithuania, Latvia and even Germany. All the children had had their schooling disrupted to various degrees and so the classes were determined by academic ability and not by age.

On his first day, Josh was assessed academically and assigned to a class. Josh had rudimentary ability in literacy from observing his brother's tutoring in the early years of the German occupation. The prevailing school system comprised four years of primary school and eight years of secondary school. Josh was moved progressively from class to class and completed primary school in his first year. By the time he left Munich in 1949, Josh had almost completed his third year of secondary school.

Yiddish proved to be the common language in which the children could be taught arithmetic, history (Jewish and general), geography, drawing and music, although the teachers would often explain things in multiple languages. The children were also taught Hebrew and English.

Josh was an avid and diligent student, liked and respected by his teachers and fellow students. He was also a regular member of the school choir. The choir performed on all the Jewish holidays and festivals, with Josh often taking a lead soloist role. For Purim he performed the role of Mordechai[26], and for Hannukah[27], he was the *shamash*. The Hannukah pageant featured eight girls from the choir

---

26 Mordechai is one of the heroes of the Purim story, which recounts the saving of the Jews of ancient Persia from annihilation. 27 Shamash: The tallest candle used to light the other eight candles of a Hannukah menorah.

dressed as candles. As the *shamash*, Josh needed to stand above them all. Unfortunately, he was still very small and had to stand on a stool to deliver his solo.

Over summer, the children were taken on school camps, once to Walchensee and once to Herreninsel, where the school would rent a small hotel for a couple of weeks. These were wonderful trips, filled with boating, swimming, hiking, singing and dancing. A celebration of life.

Josh's favourite aspect of school was the soccer team. He had never played before but picked up the skills with ease. He loved the discipline of training, the excitement of matches and the camaraderie of the team environment. The school team was affiliated with the Maccabi (Jewish sports) organisation.

The coach of Josh's team played for Bayern Munich, one of the highest ranked and most famous German teams, and also for the German national team. Josh and his new soccer friends, Mark Sperling and Zvi Lefkovic, took the tram to the stadium at Grunwald every Saturday to watch their coach play. Two Munich-based teams competed in the Suddeutscher Oberliga (the South Germany Upper League), Bayern Munich and 1860 Munich, so there was a home game every week.

ALIYAH

> **'And if anyone should survive, do not stay on this land soaked with Jewish blood—go to Palestine.'**
> SOLOMON PILA, DECEMBER 1943, SRODULA GHETTO, POLAND

* * *

Although life in Munich was relatively good for Josh and others in the Jewish community, the city was still effectively a transit camp. Few Jews had any intention of staying for very long.

Bronia and Isaac wanted to go to America. It was far away from the ruins and conflicts of Europe, and two of Isaac's sisters had already obtained permits to move there. Josh's uncles, Usher, Victor and Karl Pila, moved to Canada. However, Josh wanted to go to Palestine. He was more inclined to adhere to the advice of his father, given to him in Srodula, than to the wishes of his stepfather. In Josh's mind, there was never any doubt that Palestine was where he belonged.

This sentiment was reinforced at his strongly Zionist school. The students sang Hebrew songs, learnt folklore and discussed nation-building, emotionally charged messages that trumped practicalities such as the economic opportunities in America.

Of course, getting to Palestine in those early post-war years was problematic. The British, who held the UN mandate over the region, prohibited and actively blocked Jewish immigration in order to appease the oil-rich Arab populations. While Jewish organisations were active in defying British restrictions and illegally smuggling European Jews into Palestine, the journey remained difficult and dangerous. Many Jews who attempted to emigrate to Palestine found themselves in camps in Cyprus, once again surrounded by barbed wire.

* * *

In 1947, a window of opportunity opened for those harbouring the Zionist dream.

After much diplomatic wrangling, a resolution to partition Palestine into a Jewish state and an Arab state was put to the UN. To pass, the resolution required a two-thirds majority of valid votes, not counting abstaining votes and absent members. The vote was always going to be close, with partition vehemently opposed by the Arab and Muslim countries and much lobbying from all sides. At one stage, the Zionist lobby had to implement strategies to delay the vote by a couple of days until they could secure the votes that they needed.

To the surprise of many, the Soviet block of countries, with one exception, voted in favour of partition. This may have been driven by Joseph Stalin's desire to drive a wedge between the USA, which was in favour of partition, and Britain, which was keen to protect its commercial interests in the Arab world and ultimately abstained from the vote. This was enough to tilt the vote in favour of the Zionists and deliver the required majority for the partition resolution to be upheld.

On 14 May 1948, the British Mandate formally ended and Israel declared its independence. The new country was immediately attacked by Arab armies from all sides. Israel's nascent army was vastly outnumbered and was short on weapons and ammunition. The war raged for the rest of 1948 and into 1949 before Israel achieved a dominant position and a ceasefire was finally reached.

"You can go to America if you want, I'm going to Israel. We have our own country now," a teenage Josh was defiant.

The debate about where to move had continued, on and off, for months. For Bronia and Isaac it was a losing battle. Josh would not relent and the declaration of independence of Israel and the end of the War of Independence tipped the argument further in his favour. These developments were like the biblical parting of the Red Sea, offering safe passage to the Promised Land.

If Bronia and Isaac had known more about the economic situation in Israel and how difficult it was to get a job, they might have had a better chance of winning the argument. But Israel, desperate for new citizens, was promoting a rosy picture of pioneers working shoulder-to-shoulder to build a new Jewish nation in their traditional homeland.

In any event, after everything they had been through together, it was unfathomable for Bronia and Josh to separate. They would all make *aliyah* and build a new home in Israel.

* * *

The declaration of Israeli independence precipitated an enormous influx of Jewish immigrants. By this stage, getting to Israel was not difficult. The country was in desperate need of immigrants to build and defend the new Jewish state and Israeli representatives visited the Jewish communities of Europe, looking for 'recruits'.

The country was also desperately short of capital. A large proportion of its finances had to be devoted to defence and to absorbing the large number of immigrants. Still, Israel prioritised building its population and offered to fund the transportation costs of Jews who wanted to settle there.

Bronia and Isaac contacted representatives of the Yishuv to arrange their move to Israel. These representatives explained how they would be transported and what they could bring. They learnt that duties on the import of goods into Israel were very high, but as immigrants they could bring goods in duty free.

Bronia, Isaac and Josh packed a container of goods to take with them. This included two Frigidaire refrigerators, three Kodak Retina range-finder cameras, Josh's bicycle, radios, a couch, beds, crockery, clothing and three Pfaff sewing machines for Isaac to use in his business as a tailor. Some of these goods were purely for resale; they knew the goods could fetch a high price in Israel.

Their journey started with a train trip from Munich to Marseilles, via Frankfurt. They stayed in Marseilles for about 10 days waiting for their ship *Atzma'ut* to be ready to sail. As per usual, Josh spent the time wandering and exploring the streets of the city.

* * *

The 360-foot long, 4,570-ton ship Atzma'ut *was previously named the* Pan Crescent. *It was one of two large ships, the other being the* Pan York, *that had been purchased by the Mossad for Aliyah Bet— an organisation established to undertake unauthorised immigration into British-controlled Palestine—in January 1947. They had previously been used for 30 years by the United Fruit Company and so had climate-controlled holds that, with some modifications, could accommodate several thousand refugees.*

In 1947, Pan Crescent *and* Pan York *were involved in a major operation organised by Mossad to transport Jewish refugees from Romania to Palestine. What followed was an epic story of diplomacy and intrigue, sabotage and daring escapes. Ultimately, when the ships sailed through the Bosphorus Strait and the Dardanelles into the Mediterranean Sea, they were escorted by British naval ships to Cyprus, where the refugees were held in internment camps.*

With Israel's independence opening the country to Jewish immigration, the newly named Atzma'ut *was back in business, ferrying Jewish refugees to their new homeland.*

* * *

Josh, Bronia and Isaac boarded *Atzma'ut* on Saturday 30 April 1949 for the six-day trip to Israel. It was not a luxury cruise liner. Passengers slept in the large hold, an open area decked out in triple layers of bunks, and ate their meals in communal sittings on the deck. However, the atmosphere on the boat was exhilarating. During their transit, they celebrated the first anniversary of Yom HaAtzma'ut, Israeli Independence Day. All the passengers and crew sang songs and made speeches long into the night. Spirits were high as the passengers excitedly spoke of what awaited them in their new home.

Josh was 14 years old and there were few passengers his age on board. He spent his time with a group of 17 and 18-year-olds, future kibbutzniks, attracted to their sense of hope and youthful optimism.

* * *

"I see land! That's *Ha Eretz. Eretz* Israel."

Spirits soared on the morning of Friday 6 May 1949, when land was finally spotted. Hundreds of Jewish refugees raced to the bow of the ship, and with hands above their eyes to block the sun, peered at the land visible on the horizon.

They laughed, they cried, they stood in silence, they broke into song. For survivors of the Holocaust, sailing into Israel was the ultimate salvation. Perhaps not since Moses lead the Israelites out of bondage in Egypt had the Promised Land promised so much.

It took several hours from the first sighting of land for the ship to make its way into the port at Haifa. Those hours were filled with songs, hugs and excited conversations.

The ship finally docked in the early afternoon. Passengers who were linked to a specific kibbutz were picked up and driven away in trucks. Others, including Josh, Bronia and Isaac, were processed by the immigration agency and taken to a holding camp just outside the small seaside town of Atlit. The camp was similar to the DP camps in Europe with tents, communal meals, wire fences and armed guards. The fences and guards were designed to protect those staying at the camp from outsiders, not to keep people in.

The next day, Josh volunteered to venture out of the camp to search for Bronia's brother, Avram Lancman. They had an address for Avram in Tel Aviv, given to them in Munich by an American officer who had befriended Avram and his daughter Sonia while in Cyprus.

Josh hitched a ride to Tel Aviv with a car full of soldiers. At least two of them were Mahal volunteers from America. During the War of Independence, and in fact throughout modern Israel's history, non-Israeli Jews could enlist in the Israel Defence Forces under the Mahal volunteer program.

The soldiers dropped Josh at the central bus station in Tel Aviv, HaTachana HaMerkazit, from where he could easily get to anywhere in the city. Unbeknownst to Josh, HaTachana HaMerkazit is in the south of Tel Aviv and the address Josh had for Avram was in the north. As Josh did not have any Israeli money to buy a bus ticket, he had to walk for nearly two hours to reach his destination at 184 Ben Yehuda Street. Unfortunately, it turned out not to be Avram's home address but his tailor shop. By that time, the shop was closed for the day and Avram had already gone home.

Not for the first time, Josh was lost and adrift. He sat on the step of the shop, contemplating what he should do next. "Can I help you? Are you looking for someone?" asked a young woman who lived in the apartment above the shop. "Yes, I'm looking for my uncle. I just arrived from Germany and I wanted to surprise him, but this is the only address I have for him. Do you know Avram Lancman?" Josh answered in a mix of Yiddish and broken Hebrew.

The woman did indeed know Avram Lancman; her family owned the building and Avram was their tenant. She ran to tell her parents and they invited Josh to stay with them until Avram arrived at the shop the next day. They shared a delicious home cooked meal and looked after him well.

The next morning, when Avram came to the shop, the landlords excitedly told him that his nephew from Germany had come to see him and was staying upstairs. Avram ran up the stairs to find Josh still fast asleep in bed.

Avram's tailor shop did not open for business that day. Instead, Avram and his daughter Sonia travelled with Josh to Atlit to visit Bronia and Isaac. It was a joyful reunion for the brother and sister. Taking markedly different routes, they found themselves reunited in the Jewish homeland, far from their family home on Dekerta Street in Sosnowiec. In the days that followed, Josh would also be reunited with his cousin, Avram's son Natan, who would become one of his closest friends in Israel.

A similarly emotional reunion took place a few days later when Bronia and Josh went to visit Eliezer, another of Bronia's brothers, who was living in Bat Yam. Eliezer had left Poland in 1920 to live in Palestine and so Eliezer and Bronia had not seen each other for close to 30 years.

IMMIGRANTS

'The State of Israel will be open for Jewish immigration and for the ingathering of the Exiles.'

DECLARATION OF THE ESTABLISHMENT OF THE STATE OF ISRAEL, 14 MAY 1948

* * *

With the Israeli Declaration of Independence in 1948 and the successful conclusion of the War of Independence in 1949, Israel had become a fully-fledged sovereign state. One of its first orders of business was the absorption of large numbers of Jewish immigrants.

In May 1948, the Jewish population of Israel numbered around 700,000. Over the next four years, Israel took in another 700,000 immigrants.[26] This rapid increase in population placed an enormous strain on the nation's budding economy. The newcomers were primarily made up, in equal parts, of Holocaust survivors from Europe and Jewish refugees from Arab/Muslim countries in the Middle East and North Africa.

The overwhelming majority of these immigrants arrived with no possessions or money. The Jews of Europe had lost everything. The Jews from Arab countries were heavily restricted in the money and possessions that they could take with them, and in any event were mostly poor to begin with.

The new state struggled under the financial pressure to provide housing, education, healthcare and jobs to its new citizens. Israel was poor, living standards were basic and tough, but, nevertheless, life was exciting and full of promise.

---

[26] 1948 – 101,828; 1949 – 239,954; 1950 – 170,563; 1951 – 175,879

With the doubling of Israel's population within the first few years of its existence, housing became a central concern of the new government. Some accommodation became available in homes vacated by Arab populations during the War of Independence. These abandoned houses were declared state property and made available for immigrant families to rent. Multiple families were often assigned to the same house, each family allocated just a single room. Even so, the stock of empty houses was exhausted by the end of 1949 and other options had to be pursued.

From 1950, the government established temporary or transitory refugee absorption camps, maabarah *settlements, to house refugees and immigrants until permanent public housing,* shikun, *could be built.*

* * *

After spending three weeks in the transit camp in Atlit, Josh, Bronia and Isaac found an abandoned Arab house adjacent to an orange grove between Jaffa and Bat Yam. Another Israeli family had settled there first and occupied the main house, so Josh and his family lived in the basement.

They sold one of the fridges they had brought from Germany to pay for some basic renovations to make the basement liveable, installing windows and doors and connecting plumbing. The home was without electricity so Josh had to do his homework by candlelight. They were also unable to use their remaining fridge and instead used an ice box to keep food cool. There was no road or footpath leading up to the home, just a sandy field that did not lend itself to bike riding. It was a long walk for Josh to the nearest ice factory to buy blocks of ice, which he carried home in large ice clamps to put in the ice box.

The family cooked their meals on a portable Primus kerosene stove, which was commonly used in homes throughout Israel.

Housing was not the only necessity in short supply during those early years in Israel. There were also significant food shortages and the government was forced to impose austerity measures. Food was heavily rationed and people were encouraged to grow their own produce wherever possible.

Once again, Josh found himself dealing with food coupons, only this time he could access them legitimately. Different food rations were assigned to people depending on their age and occupation.

ISAAC, JOSH, BRONIA, JOSH'S COUSIN & BEST FRIEND NATAN LANCMAN, AVRAM LANCMAN, TEL AVIV, 1949

Some foods were readily available, such as bread and certain fruits including *sabras*—a type of prickly pear—pomegranates, figs, many varieties of oranges and mandarins. Other foods, such as meat and sausages, were hard to come by and very expensive. The use of substitutes was pervasive, fruit peel was used to make tea and traditional liver pate was made from eggplants. A form of accounting was roughly applied to different food groups; seven olives were considered nutritionally equivalent to an egg and seven eggs nutritionally equivalent to a steak.

Shortly after moving into the new house, Isaac went to the market and bought a tray of 100 baby chicks. The family set up a heater in one of the rooms of the basement to keep them warm. The chickens snuggled up to each other, looking like a plush yellow carpet that got bigger every day as they grew. Once a week they would kill one of the roosters to provide meat and make chicken soup by boiling the bones. They kept the hens for eggs.

Alongside the house, they sectioned off a small part of a sand dune and converted it into a vegetable garden. They used chicken manure as fertiliser and built a fence to keep out hyenas. In addition to the chickens, they also had ducks and turkeys.

After 18 months in the basement of the house in the orange grove, the family rented a shop in a small nearby shopping strip where Isaac conducted his tailoring business. To help reduce costs, they lived on the premises, partitioning a small living space in the back of the shop with a curtain.

They had applied for public housing when they first moved into the house in the orange grove, so in 1952 they secured a house in a *shikun,* one of the earlier housing projects in Bat Yam, close to the city centre. They were assigned one of four small basic apartments in a two-storey building. The other apartments housed a Bulgarian family, an Egyptian family and a Yemenite family comprising a man, his two wives and their six children.

* * *

Bat Yam ('daughter of the sea') is a city on the central coast just south of Tel Aviv and Jaffa. It was founded in 1926 under its original name, Bayit va-Gan ('house and garden'), and received local council status in 1937, when its name was changed to Bat Yam.

In the period following independence, Bat Yam had one of the highest intakes of immigrants of any town in Israel. Its population of 1000 inhabitants in 1948 grew to about 10,000 in 1953, with immigrants from Iraq, Libya, Egypt and Morocco living alongside those from Romania, Poland and Bulgaria.

It was a relatively poor neighbourhood. In the early 1950s, only four residents owned a motor car and no more than a dozen homes had a telephone. The social elite, the more well-to-do establishment class, were the drivers, and part owners, of the bus company. The town had a village atmosphere where everyone knew all their neighbours and most residents commuted to Tel Aviv or Jaffa for work.

* * *

Josh enrolled at a school named Bayit VaGan in Year 8. The teachers wanted Josh, who was 15 years old, to start in a lower grade because he did not speak Hebrew. Josh and Bronia were keen that he attend school with children closer to his own age, so he took private lessons to improve his language skills to an acceptable level.

Bat Yam was a very traditional community and the school had a religious orientation. Josh was not at all observant, but he saw this education as an opportunity to develop an understanding about what it meant to be Jewish. He also hoped to develop insight into why, historically, Jews always seemed to be persecuted.

Josh's classmates were mostly locals, rather than refugee immigrants like himself. They were the children of Zionist pioneers who had carved out a community in the tough conditions of Palestine, who had learned to fight to defend themselves, first from the periodic attacks from their Arab neighbours and then through the existential threat of the War of Independence. This breed of Israeli youth grew up tough and combative.

His fellow students had little sympathy for the ordeal Josh had gone through during the Holocaust. They had no concept of what it had taken for Josh to survive. They couldn't understand how the Jews of Europe had allowed themselves to be led to their deaths like lambs to the slaughter.

"Why didn't you fight them," they taunted Josh, "we would never have let them do that to us." They gave no concession to the fact that Josh had only been five years old when Germany invaded. They called him "soap", a reference to stories that the Nazis had manufactured soap out of human fat. Josh had to fight the boy leading these taunts, wrestling him to the ground and pressing his face into the dirt, in order to win the respect of the other children.

After this bumpy start, Josh's school life was extremely positive. He developed many strong and lasting friendships, had inspirational teachers, and loved his lessons.[27]

During Josh's first year at the school, a student was expelled for slapping his English teacher. Without finishing Year 8, the last year of compulsory schooling, this student would have found it very hard to get a job. Despite being new to the school and the community, Josh felt motivated to advocate for his classmate and joined a delegation of students to meet with the headmaster. The headmaster refused to revoke his decision. Josh and the other members of the delegation then organised a strike of all the students in that year. They refused to

---

27 Several of his school cohort went on to have highly successful careers, including one student who became an admiral in the navy and others who held high positions or won distinguished awards.

come back to school until the expelled student was reinstated. Eventually, the headmaster relented and gave the boy another chance. Josh's Year 8 certificate states: "Joshua excels in the core of his studies but allows himself to disregard the rules of the school, which we will not tolerate."

After that first year of school, Josh dropped out. The remaining four years of high school were neither compulsory nor free. He did not believe that his family could afford to pay school fees, and he wanted to earn money to contribute to the family finances.

In 1950, Josh started a clerking job at a bank in Tel Aviv. His role mostly involved delivering paperwork to branches of other banks to settle inter-bank transactions. He worked in that job for over a year.

After his stint in the workforce, Josh's former maths teacher and the school headmaster pushed for him to return to school. They felt that Josh was too strong a student to miss out on an education. The headmaster approached Bronia and came to an arrangement in relation to school fees. Josh returned to school in Year 10 having missed Year 9 altogether.

Throughout his school years in Israel, Josh pursued his love of soccer. He played with his mates at every opportunity, often using rolled up socks as a ball. Josh developed a reputation in Bat Yam as a skilled soccer player.

He joined the Hapoel Tel Aviv junior team, one of the top junior teams in Israel. Some of his teammates went on to represent Israel in the national team. Several times a week, Josh rode his bicycle to the club's grounds in Jaffa, where they trained and played home games. For away games, the team would travel by bus from Jaffa.

His soccer skills gave Josh instant status amongst his peers and added significantly to his sense of belonging.

*JOSH WAS FAST-TRACKED TO THE RANK OF OFFICER
IN THE ISRAELI DEFENCE FORCES*

ARMY

From the outset, the Israel Defence Force (IDF) has been central to Israeli society. Surrounded by powerful and hostile enemies, a strong defence capability has been essential for Israel's survival. With a policy of mandatory conscription at the age of 18, serving in the army is a rite of passage for Israeli youth, an integral part of growing up in the Jewish homeland.

* * *

When Josh finished his final year of school in May 1954, he was subject to immediate conscription into the army. Josh decided however that he wanted to defer his army service until he had completed tertiary studies in engineering. The army would pay his university fees along with a small living allowance, and, after graduating, he would join the army with an officer's rank. However, it also meant that he had to commit to army service for much longer than the mandatory three years.

Josh had to meet two key requirements to defer his army service until after his university studies. He had to be accepted by his chosen academic institution, the Technion in Haifa, and he had to undergo psychometric testing to establish that he was officer material.

The extensive tests, conducted over six days, involved teamwork, problem solving and dealing with a range of different situations.

Participants were divided into groups of 10 and asked to complete difficult tasks like crossing a creek or manoeuvring over a high wall with limited equipment. For each task, a different participant was appointed as the team leader and their leadership capabilities were assessed. In other activities, the participants were shown pictures and asked to write a story based on the images. These were then used as the basis for group discussions about politics and ethics.

A psychologist and a psychiatrist were allocated to each test group, day and night, for the entire time, to monitor and observe their conduct and how they behaved and interacted even when not being tested. Josh found the tests to be intensive but satisfying, even uplifting. He scored highly and his application to defer his army service was approved.

Josh was required to complete three months of basic army training before entering university. Basic training was conducted at the training camp Bahad 4, in an old British army base called Sarafand, south-east of Tel Aviv. Training was primarily focused on fitness, marching and weaponry. Josh learned to clean, disassemble, reassemble and fire a Mauser rifle (supplied by Czechoslovakia), an FN machine gun (supplied by Belgium), a Sten machine gun, and a Mills hand grenade.

Toward the end of Josh's basic training, Bronia and Isaac informed him that they were moving to Australia. They had experienced great difficulty making ends meet in Israel given the tough economic conditions. They had originally gone to Israel for Josh, but now that he had finished school and settled into his army service it was time to move on. Bronia's sister, Fela, was already in Australia and was able to help them obtain visas.

After all they had endured together, separating from Bronia was heart-wrenching for Josh. They had always been a team but now

*JOSH WITH HIS MOTHER, BRONIA, & STEPFATHER,
ISAAC LEVIT IN ISRAEL, C. 1954*

they would be on opposite sides of the world. Josh decided that he no longer wanted to defer his army service. Instead, he would complete the mandatory three-year service straight away and keep his options open as to what he would do after that, including the possibility of joining Bronia and Isaac in Australia. Josh advised the army of his change of plans.

At the end of basic training, each new recruit is assigned to an army unit. However, because Josh had earlier applied to defer his service, he hadn't been allocated to a unit. The administration had not caught up with his change of plans and needed to consider what to do with him. On reviewing Josh's file, they noted his high scores when assessed for officer potential. They were also aware that his pre-service medical established that he was unfit for combat duties. The examining doctor had detected a heart murmur and sent him to a specialist clinic where five elderly German doctors listened to his heart for about an hour. There was a definite murmur which they concluded had been caused by a four-week bout of severe rheumatic fever in Munich in 1947 that had rendered Josh unable to walk. He had developed the illness after playing a soccer match on a cold wet day and not drying off. A common complication of rheumatic fever is damage to heart valves, resulting in a murmur.[28]

So, faced with a young man with leadership potential but medically fit only for a desk job, the IDF decided to fast track Josh through the officer training courses, awarding him officer status in unusually quick time.

* * *

The next step in Josh's army training was the infantry sergeant training, a three-month course conducted at Bahad 3. Here, Josh was trained in more advanced weapons, medical first-aid and leadership.

---

[28] Interestingly, when tested in Melbourne many years later, Josh was found to no longer have a murmur. The damage to his heart valves had rectified itself.

While Bahad 3 is located in Netanya, Josh spent most of his time at a smaller base in the Jerusalem hills. This included regular night training patrols of the area. On one of these patrols, on the eve of Passover 1955, Josh's group was surprised to hear rustling in the bushes. Soon after, shots were fired in their direction. They had encountered a group of Arab raiders who had stolen across the border.

It was a pitch-black night and they could not see their adversaries. Without hesitation, Josh knelt on one knee, as he had been trained, and fired his rifle in the direction of the enemy. Several volleys of shots rang out and a bullet struck a rock behind Josh and ricocheted into his calf.

With adrenaline surging through his system, Josh initially did not feel the wound. He did however notice blood seeping onto his leg and trousers and called for medical assistance. An inexperienced medic came to his assistance but nearly passed out at the sight of so much blood. Josh had to take the sterile bandage from the medic and bandage his own wound.

With the skirmish over, Josh limped back to base. He was sent to the hospital in Sarafand where his leg was x-rayed. The doctors determined that it was safer to leave the bullet in his calf than to try and remove it and it has remained there ever since.

The wound put Josh out of action for only three days and, anxious not to worry his mother, he decided to never tell Bronia that he had been injured by gunfire.

* * *

The final step in Josh's training was the most intensive—a six-month officers' course at Bahad 1 in Pardes Chana, just east of the town of Hadera. Each morning that they were on base, approximately two weeks out of every month, they woke at 5.20am and ran the eight kilometres each way to Hadera train station and back. The course included off-base field training and on-base lectures on the theories of war delivered by different senior officers. At the end of the course, Josh was promoted to the rank of second lieutenant, with a ceremony held on base in August 1955.

With his training complete, Josh took a job in the manpower department (unit 50) at the major army base between Ramat Gan and Bnei Brahk, east of Tel Aviv. Unit 50 received reports from combat units regarding casualties. If a soldier had been killed, the applicable city officer would be then responsible for informing the soldier's family before names could be broadcast on the radio. Unit 50 would also liaise with army units regarding their requirements for new personnel to replace casualties.

Josh was the junior officer in unit 50, reporting to a more senior officer. He held that position throughout the significant events of 1956, including the Sinai Campaign, the military operation in late October in which the IDF invaded the Sinai Peninsula as part of a joint operation with England and France to reclaim control of the Suez Canal.

* * *

In the period between 1949 and 1956, there were numerous Arab incursions into Israeli territory and murderous attacks on Israeli citizens. The attacks largely came out of Egyptian-controlled Gaza and the Jordanian-controlled West Bank, with the active support of those two countries. These attacks were deliberately targeted at civilians; hundreds were killed and many more wounded. They caused considerable disruption to Israeli communities close to the borders and anguish and outrage amongst the Israeli population more generally.

Because of the clandestine and random nature of the incursions, it was not possible for the Israeli government to stop them completely.

Instead, the government implemented a policy of reprisal actions intended as a form of deterrence—to impose a high cost for the spilling of Israeli blood.

In the period leading up to the Sinai Campaign, one such action, codenamed Operation Samaria, was conducted on 10 October 1956 against the Qalqilya police station in the north-west of the West Bank, close to the Israeli border. The action was in retaliation for two attacks by Palestinian fedayeen militants from Jordan.

* * *

Like most reprisal actions, Operation Samaria was conducted at night. On arriving in the office the next morning, Josh asked his staff for the casualty reports. His staff equivocated, telling him that the reports hadn't come in yet. When they couldn't justify delaying any longer, they handed him the list.

Josh scanned his eyes down the list of names of soldiers that were reported killed. Thirteen young Israelis had lost their lives fighting for their country.

Josh's heart dropped as his eyes locked onto the name Natan Lancman, his first cousin, Avram's son, and his best friend. He sat in stunned disbelief, overcome with grief, while his staff hovered around him not knowing what to say or do.

Josh was familiar with the process when a soldier was killed in combat. Once the family had been informed, a counselling session would be arranged for the parents with people who had previously lost a child, to help them with their grief.

Although Josh was devastated, he knew that he needed to be with his aunt and uncle, Natan's parents, to support them in their grief. He took a car from the car pool and headed to their home. Somehow, he got there before the city officer. Initially, they were pleasantly surprised to see him in the middle of the day, but knowing the responsibilities of his job and recalling that there had been a battle the night before, they quickly realised that his presence could only mean the worst of all possible news. They all broke down and cried.

Meanwhile, back at unit 50, Josh's team was trying to reconcile an anomaly. On the one hand, they had the report of the 13 soldiers killed in the Qalqilyah action. On the other hand, they had a separate report of an initial 12 bodies received at the morgue. Frantic phone calls to field officers helped them piece together what had happened.

During the action at Qalqilyah, a Jordanian soldier had tossed a grenade into an Israeli half-track armoured vehicle, killing all of those on board. Natan had not been in the vehicle but fighting on foot nearby. He was shot in the thigh. The bullet had struck him in the pocket of his fatigues, where he kept his spare ammunition. The bullets in his pocket exploded, significantly damaging his leg. Virtually unable to move, he had crawled into the bombed out half-track and hidden among the bodies of his dead comrades.

As the Israeli unit pulled back, they took note of who was with them and who had not returned. It was on this basis that Natan was reported as being among the dead. In accordance with the IDF mantra that no soldier, dead or alive, is to be left behind, the Israelis re-engaged with the Jordanian forces to recover the bodies of their fallen colleagues. During this recovery action, another five Israeli soldiers were killed. In the confusion, the Israelis found that they had one more person in hospital than they had accounted for, and one less body in the morgue. Natan Lancman was seriously wounded—but alive!

A military police vehicle, sirens blaring, was sent to the Lancman's house with the news. Josh and his aunt and uncle listened in disbelief as they heard that Natan was alive, and then hugged each other with tears streaming down their faces. Their relief quickly turned to concern when they heard how badly he had been injured.

At the time of the Qalqilyah action, Natan had only a few months left of army service. Natan's wounds were significant and he did not see combat duty again. He did, however, recover well and go on to raise a family, before sadly passing away from a heart attack in his forties.

SAFE HARBOUR

After many years navigating the stormy seas of war-torn Europe and the volatile Middle East, Josh drifted away from the main stream of history and into the calm waters and safe harbour of Melbourne, Australia.

* * *

As his army service was coming to a close, Josh was approached by a senior officer wanting to recruit him into the army intelligence unit. This officer appreciated Josh's sharp intellect and analytical skills, as well as his proficiency in many languages, and thought he would be perfect for such a role. The offer was attractive to Josh but would have involved him signing up to another 15 years in the army, which he could not commit to.

Bronia and Isaac had moved to Australia two years earlier and Josh missed his mother terribly. Having shared such hardships, he owed it to her to make every effort to be together.

Josh felt very strongly that he belonged in Israel and had always envisioned that the country would be his long-term home. However, to be closer to his mother, Josh decided to undertake his university studies in Melbourne, Australia. The problem was that student visas were difficult to acquire. Bronia consulted an immigration lawyer in Melbourne but he was unable to make any headway.

Reminiscent of the time she went to the Sosnowiec police station to advocate for the release of Solomon's brothers, Bronia flew to Canberra and went, without an appointment, to the Department of Immigration, where she insisted on seeing the minister for immigration, Athol Townley. Government ministers are not in the habit of accepting impromptu meetings from members of the public and Townley's staff tried to redirect Bronia to the usual application channels. Bronia, however, refused to accept no for an answer.

Eventually her perseverance paid off and she was granted a 10-minute audience with the minister. Those few minutes were all she needed. The minister was so moved by Bronia's story that when he emerged from the meeting he instructed his staff to send an urgent telegraph to the Australian embassy in Israel directing that a visa be issued to Josh without delay. One condition of his Australian visa was to undergo an official medical examination before his arrival. He would have had to wait months for an examiner endorsed by the Australian authorities to do this in Israel, but he could hasten the process by having the examination in Rome.

Josh sold the apartment in Bat Yam to the Yemenite neighbours and flew to Italy. Due to Israeli restrictions on money taken out of the country, he arrived in Rome with just $US10. He spent $2.40 on duty free cigarettes and a further $5 on his bus fare into Rome. This left him with just $2.60 for his month in the city. Josh asked his uncle Karl, who was living in Canada, to forward him a further $US100 which he had to spend sparingly. He stayed in the cheapest accommodation he could find and ate one very cheap pasta meal, purchased from a street food vendor, each day. He spent his days walking the streets of Rome which he came to know very well.

The medical exam revealed that Josh had, in his childhood, suffered from tuberculosis, the disease that had killed his sister Rachel. It is likely that they had both contracted the disease during their time hiding in the bunker in Srodula.

During his time in Rome, Josh travelled to Munich to collect money from the sale of the Bat Yam apartment. As he was not allowed to take money out of Israel, he had arranged to collect the proceeds in Germany. In Munich, at a restaurant with some Jewish American soldiers that he had met on a train, Josh was mistaken for Horst Buchholz, at the time one of Germany's most famous film actors, known as the 'German James Dean'. Josh had never heard of Horst Buchholz but was pleased to accept the special attention and free meal and champagne that came with this mistaken identity.

Josh flew from Munich to Rome to collect his Australian visa and then, with much excitement, he boarded a plane to Melbourne. As was typical at that time, the journey from Europe to Australia took several days. This route included overnight stopovers in Karachi, Ceylon and Singapore and a stop in Darwin for breakfast. Josh travelled economy class but found the hotels he was put up in at each stopover to be quite luxurious.

Finally, in October 1957, Josh arrived in Melbourne. He travelled by bus from the airport to the house that Bronia and Isaac shared with another family in Osborne Street, South Yarra. Bronia had organised a big reunion party for Josh, attended by Fela and her daughters, Augustine and Rosalie, and several of Bronia's new friends.

Josh applied to study architecture at the University of Melbourne. He was accepted into the course based on his Israeli matric and an informal oral English exam. One of the lecturers spoke to him for half an hour to assess his English language skills; they spoke mostly about the political situation in the Middle East and water scarcity problems in the region.

Josh had to pay fees for his first year of university, but thereafter was awarded scholarships that enabled him to study for free. He supported himself with numerous part-time jobs, including house painting, working in the warehouse of a wholesaling business, and teaching Hebrew.

Once again, Josh embarked on a fresh beginning, a new life in a new country, in this case a country far removed, physically and culturally, from the life he left behind.

JOSH MET THE LOVE OF HIS LIFE, MARY, WHILE STUDYING ARCHITECTURE AT THE UNIVERSITY OF MELBOURNE

MARY

Josh was chatting with his good friend Tuvye at Melbourne University one day. Josh and Tuvye had met earlier in the year on the number 8 tram, travelling along Toorak Road. Despite maintaining a low profile about his background, Josh wore an Israeli platoon commander badge on his lapel, a badge that was meaningless to most people but was immediately recognisable to fellow Israelis as signifying that the wearer had completed the IDF officers' training course. Tuvye, himself a veteran of the Israeli army, recognised the badge and struck up a conversation that led to a lifelong friendship.

At uni, Josh pointed out an attractive fellow architecture student, Mary Joan Lloyd, who had caught his eye. "She's Jewish, you know," Tuvye told him with a glint in his eye.

The School of Architecture was at the time housed in temporary army barracks on the university campus. In addition to lecture theatres and drawing rooms, the centrepiece of the building was a large foyer. Here students would mill around, meeting classmates and viewing other students' projects that were displayed on a rotational basis.

Josh had met Mary in the foyer on several occasions. Despite being several years younger than Josh, Mary was two years ahead of him in the course. Josh was very pleased to receive an invitation to

Mary's 20th birthday party in July of 1958. It was the first stanza in a blossoming romance that would lead to a marriage for the ages.

As he got to know her, Josh discovered that, despite her anglicised name, Mary was born in Romania and was herself a victim of displacement due to the Holocaust.

* * *

Mary's parents were Leon and Lily Leibovici. Leon was born on 13 February 1895 in the small town of Stefanesti in the county of Botosani, in the far north-east of Romania, close to what is now the border with Moldova. Botosani had a sizeable Jewish community dating back several hundred years. Leon's father was employed to manage the properties of a local non-Jewish landlord. His uncle was a prominent rabbi.

After finishing high school in 1913, Leon studied engineering (general machine construction) at the Technical University (*Technische Hochschule*) in Charlottenburg, Berlin. Studying at a university in Romania at the time was either not permitted or was too dangerous for Jewish students who were regularly beaten.

Leon was still in Berlin in 1916 when Romania entered World War I on the side of the Allies. Considered an enemy alien to the Germans, Leo was interned in a prisoner-of-war camp at Holzminden, Hannover.

When World War I ended, Leon resumed his studies, completing them in 1922. He then returned to Romania and took a job as a technical salesman in Bucharest with a firm called Societea Continentala Pentru Comertul Fierului, Kern & Co, a subsidiary sales organisation for a large Czechoslovakian iron and steel producer called Witkowitz Iron and Steel Works.

In Bucharest, Leon met Lily Jacobson. Lily and her sister Henrietta came from a middle-class family, their father owned a

MARY'S PARENTS LEON & LILY LEIBOVICI, EARLY 1930s

large hardware store. Lily had undertaken a law degree at the university in Bucharest, but did so almost entirely from home, with the assistance of tutors, to avoid the virulent anti-Semitism on campus.

Leon and Lily were married in 1930. Leon rose to the higher ranks in the Romanian branch of Witkowitz Iron and Steel Works, and his income afforded Leon and Lily a life of adventure and travel. They visited countries all over Europe and the Middle East and spent weekends skiing and hiking in the mountains closer to home.

In July 1938, Leon and Lily welcomed their only child, Mary.

* * *

There is a long Jewish history in the region that became Romania, dating back to at least the second century AD. In more recent times, Jews in Romania suffered expulsions and persecution, pogroms and discrimination, reminiscent of the anti-Semitism Jews experienced in Poland and elsewhere in Eastern Europe. Jews were treated as second-class citizens at best, if they were legally considered to be citizens at all.

Romania was in political turmoil when Ion Antonescu came to power in 1940 at the beginning of World War II. He was keenly focused on the recovery of territories that Romania had previously lost to Hungary, Bulgaria and Ukraine. To this end, he joined the Axis alliance, which promised to deliver him the territories that he passionately believed rightfully belonged to Romania.

Antonescu shared many of Hitler's views on racial purification and the role of Jews in the rise of Bolshevism in the Soviet Union. He too was intent on ridding his society of Jews. However, while Romania was allied to, and fought alongside, Nazi Germany for most of the wartime period, the country was not occupied by the Germans and not subject to direct German governance and control.

Accordingly, the Holocaust in Romania followed its own unique course, dictated by Romania's historical and political context and the attitudes of Antonescu and the ruling elite. Antonescu's regime feared the economic ramifications of removing Jews from commercial life in Bucharest and other major cities. Also, after 1942, it became apparent to Antonescu that Nazi Germany was going to lose the war and he began to position himself for post-war peace negotiations with the Allies.

Approximately half the Jews living in Romania, or territories controlled by Romania, were murdered in the Holocaust, a death toll of some 300,000 people. However, incidents of ethnic cleansing were not evenly spread across the country. Most of those killed lived in the borderland areas or territories that were taken over by Romania during its participation in Operation Barbarossa, such as Bessarabia, Transnistria and Northern Transylvania.

While the Jews living in pre-war Romania, including the capital Bucharest, were heavily persecuted, they were not herded into ghettos or subjected to mass killing. Romania did not adopt the Final Solution implemented by Nazi Germany and did not participate in the wholesale deportation of Jews to the extermination camps in Poland.

* * *

Leon and Lily watched with rising concern as the dark storm clouds descended over Europe. In quick succession, Nazi Germany annexed Austria and Czechoslovakia, occupied half of Poland, invaded Denmark, Norway, Belgium, Holland and France and commenced bombing raids on Great Britain.

Leon and Lily were well aware of the precarious position of Jews in Romania reflected in the anti-Jewish policies, introduced from late 1940; the persecution and beating of Jews that had become commonplace; and a significant pogrom against the Jews in January 1941.

The Witkowitz Iron and Steel Works had been owned by the Rothschild family, extremely wealthy bankers and financiers, since 1843. During the 19th century, they became involved in building railways and made the strategic decision to purchase their own steel supplier.

Louis Rothschild missed his opportunity to leave Austria before Germany annexed the country into the Third Reich in 1938. He was imprisoned by the Germans for over a year, before his family finally brokered a deal for his release, which included the transfer of ownership of Witkowitz Iron and Steel Works to Nazi Germany.

* * *

After 18 years working at Witkowitz Iron and Steel Works, Leon's job was terminated in October 1940 for purely anti-Semitic reasons. A company gazette announced that Leon Leibovici, the Jew, would be replaced by an Aryan.

The future for Jews in Romania looked bleak and Leon and Lily began making plans to leave. They were keen to immigrate to Australia where Leon's younger sister Sofia and her husband, Isaac Tulcinsky, had moved in 1939. They had arranged Australian visas around the same time but had delayed their departure, in part due to difficulties in getting a permit to transit through Russia.

On 10 April 1941, Leon and Lily took their young daughter and left their home without telling anyone other than close family, and with only the belongings they could carry. They bribed the border guards to let them cross into Russia, took a train to Moscow and then the Trans-Siberian Railway to Vladivostok, a trip of over 9000 kilometres that lasted several weeks.

Their timing was impeccable. Just two months later, on 22 June 1941, Germany launched Operation Barbarossa, a massive surprise invasion of Russia and the largest German military operation of World War II. From that point on, it would no longer have been possible for Leon, Lily and Mary to cross the border from Romania into Russia or to use the Trans-Siberian Railway to take them out of harm's way.

* * *

The Trans-Siberian Railway connects Moscow with the Russian Far East and is the longest railway line in the world. Prior to Operation Barbarossa, the railway network was used extensively to ferry Japanese rubber westwards to Germany, and Jews and others eastward away from the Nazis.

With the commencement of Operation Barbarossa, the Trans-Siberian Railway was significantly repurposed to ferry Russian soldiers from the east to fight the invading Germans on Russia's western borders, and to relocate Russian factories and other businesses east, out of reach of the invaders.

* * *

From Vladivostok, the Leibovici family travelled by ship to Shanghai where they stayed for a few weeks before another ship took them to Japan in May 1941. In Yokohama, the port of Tokyo, they stayed in a hotel for three months waiting for their Australian visas to come through. Finally, in September 1941, the small family boarded the ocean liner *Boissevain* for the journey from Yokohama to Melbourne, arriving in Williamstown on 9 October 1941, six months after leaving their home in Romania.

Again, their timing could not have been better. Their voyage was the last passenger trip that the *Boissevain* undertook before being co-opted into military duties, ferrying the war-wounded across the Pacific Ocean. Two months after their arrival, on

7 December 1941, Japan launched a surprise attack on the US naval base at Pearl Harbor, bringing the US into the war in the Pacific and shutting down civilian shipping in the region for many years to come.

* * *

In an attempt to better integrate into Australian society, the family changed its name to the anglicised 'Lloyd', but life was challenging during the war years in Melbourne. As Romania was at the time allied with the Germans, Leon once again found himself labelled an illegal alien and subject to restrictions. He was not allowed to possess a shortwave radio or to speak a foreign language on the telephone. He was also required to get a job helping the Australian war effort, failing which he would be interned in a detention camp. He took a job at Bruck Mills, a textile company based in Wangaratta which manufactured fabric for army uniforms and blankets. He worked there until the end of the war, after which he set up his own business.

Other than Leon having permission to travel to Wangaratta and stay there from Monday to Friday, the family was heavily restricted in its movement around Melbourne, so Mary had to spend her primary school years at a local boys' school in Camberwell within walking distance from home. Later, she successfully completed her secondary school years at Fintona Girls' School, a prestigious school in Balwyn where Mary, a Romanian Jewish immigrant, did not feel entirely comfortable.

After completing her schooling, Mary went on to study architecture at Melbourne University where she had her fateful meeting with Josh.

At the time of writing, the couple have been married for six decades and continue to bring each other much joy.

JOSH & MARY'S WEDDING DAY, 1961

MARY & JOSH, CIRCA 1964

ISRAEL LANCMAN WITH BRONIA (WIFE OF AVRAM), AVRAM LANCMAN & THEIR CHILDREN SONIA & NATAN, CYPRUS 1947

THE LANCMANS

Just a few minutes' walk from the Brandenburg Gate, in the very heart of Berlin, is the Memorial to the Murdered Jews of Europe. Designed by architect Peter Eisenman, the memorial comprises 2711 grey concrete slabs of different heights, set out in an array across undulating ground on a large city block. The effect is to draw visitors, deeper and deeper, until they feel trapped, overwhelmed, surrounded by powerful forces against which they cannot fight. It is a stark and solemn place.

But the real treasure is underground in the memorial's information centre. This museum does not bombard the visitor with the horrors of the Holocaust like the museums in Auschwitz and elsewhere. Rather, it is focused on personal stories. The Room of Families tracks the fate of the members of 15 families, in different parts of Europe, to illustrate the many different ways that the Holocaust impacted people's lives.

The message here is important. History can incorporate a multitude of different stories. It is these collective experiences that define historical times.

Popular culture can create a dominant narrative of history, so that it appears that events were experienced in the same way by everyone who lived through them. The stories depicted in a multitude of Holocaust movies and books may lead observers to equate the Holocaust with internment in a concentration camp, such as Auschwitz, resulting in either death in the gas chambers or miraculous survival against the odds. In fact, alongside these resonant stories, was a vast array of different experiences of the Holocaust, more numerous than the concrete blocks in the Berlin memorial.

Tracking the fate of the Lancman family, Bronia's many siblings, provides a similar window on history. It does not cover every pathway, but a diverse range of experiences that are illustrative of the collective Jewish story.

Menasche (Bronia's brother – born 1901)

Menasche was the oldest of the siblings and was considered by all to be a genius. As a boy he was invited to study at the highly prestigious Lomza Yeshiva. He declined and instead taught himself French in anticipation of an extended visit to Paris.

Menasche lived in his wife's hometown of Bedzin and had two daughters. He and his wife ran a small café that sold beer and frankfurts.

During the war, Menasche and his family were moved into the Bedzin ghetto, which was adjacent to Sosnowiec's Srodula ghetto. Josh recalls visiting them before the ghetto was closed. When the ghetto was liquidated in July/August 1943, Menasche and his family were sent to Auschwitz and murdered in the gas chambers.

Eliezer (Bronia's brother – born 1902)

As a youth, Eliezer became infatuated with the Zionist movement. In 1920, he joined a group of like-minded Zionists to train themselves in the skills they would need to settle in Palestine and build a new nation.

Many young Zionists studied agriculture so that they could cultivate their new homeland. Eliezer learnt carpentry skills so that he could make his contribution as a builder.

In 1921, he was part of a group of pioneers that set off on the land route to Palestine, travelling through the Balkans, Turkey and Syria, and arriving in the Promised Land in 1922.

Eliezer became entrenched in Israeli life, both before and after independence. He was a project manager for Solel Bonei, the large union construction company, building *kibbutzim* and *shikkunim* (large public housing estates). He married twice and had three children.

Avram (Bronia's brother – born 1904)

Avram moved to Danzig, a town on the Baltic Sea in the north of Poland, in the early 1930s to pursue a career as a tailor with his uncle who was already established there. Over many years, Avram became a highly successful tailor.

Danzig was one of the first cities invaded and occupied by the Germans at the very beginning of World War II.

To escape persecution by the Nazis, in 1940, Avram, together with his wife, also named Bronia, and children, Sonia and Natan, boarded one of three ships that set sail for Palestine. At that time, the Nazis encouraged such emigration which removed Jews from Europe and caused headaches for the British in Palestine.

Before reaching the coast of Palestine, Avram contracted typhoid and was taken off the ship and admitted to a hospital in Cyprus.

The three ships were intercepted by the British just off the coast of Palestine. The British were concerned about upsetting the local Arab population and decided to transport the Jewish refugees to Mauritius and Trinidad. To this end, many of the refugees, including Bronia, Sonia and Natan were moved to another ship, named the *SS Patria*.

Local Zionist underground organisations in Palestine were determined to stop the *SS Patria* from transporting the Jewish refugees to faraway British colonies. A Jewish worker at the port of Haifa planted a bomb on the ship with the intent of disabling it so that the refugees would have to be brought ashore. However, he greatly miscalculated the impact of the bomb which, instead of just disabling the motor, blew a hole in the hull that caused the *SS Patria* to sink. Approximately 200 refugees, together with crew members and British soldiers, drowned. The remainder, including Bronia, Sonia and Natan, were rescued and taken ashore to Haifa.

The British determined that all survivors of the disaster who had been brought ashore would be entitled to stay in Palestine. However, this did not include Avram, who had been in hospital in Cyprus when the *SS Patria* sank and was subsequently transported to the British colony in Nyasaland (now Malawi but then part of Rhodesia). Bronia, Sonia and Natan elected not to stay in Palestine but rather to join Avram in Nyasaland.

Avram became a highly successful and sought-after tailor to the British elite in Rhodesia. He used his connections with the British powerbrokers to secure a move for him and his family to Cyprus, living in Nicosia, where he again became a very popular tailor for the British elite. The family moved to Israel shortly after Israeli independence.

Bronia (born 1906)

Fela (Bronia's sister – born 1907)

Fela was creative and an excellent dress designer and maker. After a brief marriage, Fela divorced and moved with her young son to Danzig to progress her career.

Fela visited Sosnowiec often and was interred in the Srodula ghetto. Her son, who was similar in age to Josh's brother Menasche, would sometimes hide in the bunker with Josh and Rachel during the early days of internment in the ghetto.

Fela and her son were taken during the actions in August 1943 and transported to Auschwitz. Her son was killed straight away but Fela was spared because her strong language skills—she was fluent in German and Polish—made her useful in camp administration.

After liberation, Fela stayed for a time in Bedzin. She then lived in Sosnowiec until around 1952. Fela married David Zycher and they had two daughters, Augustine and Rosalie. They ran a business manufacturing quilts.

Fela and her family then moved to Australia, sponsored by a cousin already living there.

Regina (Bronia's sister – born 1908)

Regina married Joseph, the older brother of Isaac Levit, and had three children. They led a modest life in Sosnowiec until they were all selected for extermination at the *punkt* on 12 August 1942 and sent to their deaths at Auschwitz.

Israel (Bronia's brother – born 1911)

Israel was powerfully built and mechanically minded.

He and his family were in the Srodula ghetto and then transported to Auschwitz. Israel survived, however his wife and son perished at the extermination camp.

In 1946, Israel decided to travel to Palestine. He became part of the *Aliyah Bet* movement, which assisted some 100,000 Jewish refugees attempting to illegally migrate to Palestine, thwarting attempts by the British to stop them. Israel travelled through Italy and then boarded a ship bound for Palestine. The ship was intercepted and he was sent to a detention camp on Cyprus. When Avram moved to Cyprus in 1947, he learned that his brother Israel was in detention there and was able to use his connections to make sure that he was looked after.

He moved to Israel at the first available possibility after the nation declared its independence and became a technician for Mekorot, the national water company.

David Flaumenbaum (Bronia's stepbrother)
David was interred in Auschwitz and miraculously survived the war there.

Leibl Flaumenbaum (Bronia's stepbrother)
Leibl left Poland in 1936 or 1937 to emigrate to Palestine. Josh's father, Solomon, through his role in the Revisionist movement, assisted in sponsoring his emigration, which fortuitously took him out of the path of the Nazis.

Moshe (Bronia's half-brother – born 1925)
Murdered during the Holocaust. No further details are known.

Sheba (Bronia's half-sister – born 1927)
Murdered during the Holocaust. No further details are known.

* * *

Sometimes, even divergent paths intersect.

In April 1952, the surviving Lancman siblings all found themselves in Israel and convened, with their respective families, at the home of Avram for a Passover *seder*. It was a magnificent feast, filled with prayers and customary foods. The highlight was the singing of the traditional Passover songs.

In every culture throughout human history, music has played a special role in raising spirits and evoking emotions. Josh was incredibly moved as he sat, transfixed, listening to the beautiful harmonies produced by his mother and her siblings. The hair on the back of his neck stood on end and his spirit soared. The years of horror they had endured had not diminished their singing voices. If anything, the pathos of their losses mixed with the joy of reuniting added further depth and soul to their song.

Israel, the base; Eliezer and Avram, the tenors; Bronia, the alto; and Fela, the soprano, sang long into the night, their different voices complementing each other perfectly. They sang to remember the good times as a family together in Sosnowiec. They sang to remember those who had been lost. They sang to celebrate their new lives. They also sang to forget, if only for a moment.

The Passover festival encapsulates the universal Jewish narrative: oppression and salvation, redemption, and a new beginning. The story is told through the written text but the most profound messages are found in the songs, the songs sung by the Lancmans in perfect harmony: *"Avadim hayinu*—We were slaves, now we are free..."

MARY & JOSH WITH THEIR CHILDREN JONATHAN, RON & JORDANA

EPILOGUE

Josh, the 'lucky one', thrived in Australia, the 'lucky country'.

Josh's life in Australia was so far removed from his early years in Silesia that he might as well have been on a different planet. He was no longer a hunted child, facing existential threats. Now he was free to live and thrive in any way he chose.

Australia certainly proved to be a land of opportunity for Josh, both professionally and personally.

After graduating from the University of Melbourne, Josh and Mary opened their own successful architecture practice, Joshua & Mary Pila Architects. They designed many houses and office buildings before specialising in schools, primarily for the Catholic Education Commission.

Later, they inherited Mary's father's ribbon factory and grew it into a large textile business. By any measure, Josh was an accomplished businessman, careful and astute, fair and always honest. He also proved himself to be a canny property and stock market investor.

The architecture practice was not the only successful partnership for Josh and Mary. They have a fairy-tale marriage and a wonderful family and homelife, with three children and nine grandchildren scattered all over the world. Family is paramount to Josh and Mary; their legacy lies in the generations that follow them.

Close friends and a love of tennis, which replaced Josh's earlier love of soccer, have rounded out a life well lived, a life that looked incredibly unlikely in those darkest of his early days.

* * *

Many Holocaust survivors are deeply traumatised by their experiences. Certainly, Bronia was haunted by her losses every day until she passed away at the age of 98 in 2004. Josh, on the other hand, has seemingly been able to compartmentalise the traumas of his past and limit the extent to which they have infiltrated his new world. He is a man of his times, always living in the moment.

Of Josh's many positive qualities, the most notable is his optimism. While he has every reason to be cynical, he is always positive, convinced that things will turn out for the best. When asked how he is by family and friends, he will invariably answer that he is "fit and well".

* * *

Still waters can act like a mirror, and although Josh always kept himself busy, the relative calm of Australia has afforded him plenty of time for reflection.

Like all of us, Josh's opinions and world views have been influenced and shaped by his own personal history:

Judaism
Josh is a proud and committed Jew. While being Jewish is a key—probably dominant—part of his identity, Josh is not at all religious. Before the German invasion, Josh grew up in a traditional Jewish home, keeping kosher and attending synagogue every Sabbath. However, from the age of five, war and the Holocaust intervened, and Josh could not accept the existence of a God that would allow such atrocities to occur.

In Israel, Josh attended a very religious high school where he intensively studied the Bible and the Talmud. He has always been attracted to the philosophical underpinning of the Talmudic teachings and Jewish literature.

Josh has always felt that, through suffering, Jews have developed great capacity for compassion.

Israel

Josh is a passionate supporter and defender of Israel and Zionism. His personal experiences taught him that it is vital that the Jews have their own country. He believes only fellow Jews can be counted on to look after their brethren, to protect them and to provide a home when they are not wanted elsewhere.

Living in Israel was therapeutic. Josh describes it as analogous to a decompression chamber for a deep-sea diver. It aided in a healthy transition from his wartime struggle for survival to life beyond.

Josh is deeply interested in news about Israel, always viewing current events through the prism of his own insights from having lived there. He is significantly more Israeli, in sentiment and perspective, than Polish.

Had things panned out differently, if Bronia and Isaac had not struggled to make ends meet, Josh could have happily lived out his life in Israel. While Josh's life in Australia has been extraordinarily rewarding, Israel is the only place he felt he completely belonged.

World War II and the Holocaust

Josh reads widely on the Holocaust and on the European theatres of World War II. Studying a history that he himself has lived, gives him a special perspective. When reading an historian's account of particular events or battles, Josh can't help but ponder how outcomes for his own family might have been different. For example, if the assassination attempt on Hitler had been successful in July 1944, or if the Russian army had not halted its progress through Poland to wait out the Warsaw Uprising, the war may have ended earlier and Josh's father Solomon and his sister Rachel may have survived.

Josh has some residual behaviours from his Holocaust experiences. He buys food in bulk, so that his pantry is always well stocked and he never runs out of supplies. He is also reticent to reveal to strangers that he is Jewish, and he is cautious and measured in everything he does.

Approach to Life

Not surprisingly, Josh's experiences have influenced his values and approach to life.

He believes in maintaining integrity in everything that he does. In his professional and business career, Josh had a reputation for being upfront and fair. Suppliers, customers, clients and colleagues trusted him implicitly. Not only does this accord with his sense of right and wrong, but he believes it brings out the best in other people.

Josh is ruled by logic in his decision making. When confronted with an issue, he thinks it through rationally to determine a solution. He is not given to impulsive choices or emotional behaviour. Having made a decision, he won't second guess it. The manner in which he survived the Holocaust taught him to trust his instincts. Consistent with this attitude, he has very few regrets, other than never learning a musical instrument and not playing more soccer.

Perhaps the unique partnership he shared with Bronia instilled in Josh the virtue of teamwork. Within his family unit, he thinks of what is best for the collective unit, rather than himself, and he puts the needs of others ahead of his own. This is a value he and Mary have imparted to their children and grandchildren.

EPILOGUE

Josh believes in planning for the future but living well along the way. For Josh, life is a journey, not a destination. He does not live beyond his means, but he can appreciate what he has. He is not in the least inclined to compare himself to others.

His father advised him to keep a low profile in order to survive the war. Josh has elevated this advice to a rule for life. He conducts himself quietly and without fanfare. He does not need to see his name in lights, preferring to fly under the radar.

Josh learnt the importance of being accepting of others. By displaying tolerance, and being open-minded, there is a greater chance it will be reciprocated. His inclination is not to judge others critically but rather to try and understand their perspective.

Most significantly, he learnt never to lose hope. With hope and courage, it is possible to overcome all obstacles.

* * *

Equipped with these philosophies, Josh has navigated the tides of history, with its continuous ebbs and flows, riding the waves and resisting the undertows. The manner in which Josh has done so shines like a guiding star, a lucky star, illuminating the way for others to chart their own course.

[LEFT] SOCCER WAS JOSH'S FAVOURITE SPORT BUT HE ALSO ENJOYED A GAME OF TENNIS [RIGHT] JOSH ENJOYED A SUCCESSFUL CAREER AS AN ARCHITECT

MARY & JOSH AT JOSH'S 50TH BIRTHDAY CELEBRATION, 1985

[ABOVE] THE NEXT GENERATION, JOSH & MARY WITH JONATHAN, JORDANA & RON [LEFT] DAVITA, JUSTINE, JONATHAN & DOMINIQUE [RIGHT] JORDANA, TAL, LIAM, RON & GUY

[OPPOSITE ABOVE] DAMIEN, JESSICA, JACKIE, SAMANTHA, RACHAEL & RON [OPPOSITE BELOW] FOUR GENERATIONS. BRONIA WITH JOSH, HER GRANDDAUGHTER JORDANA & GREAT GRANDSON LIAM

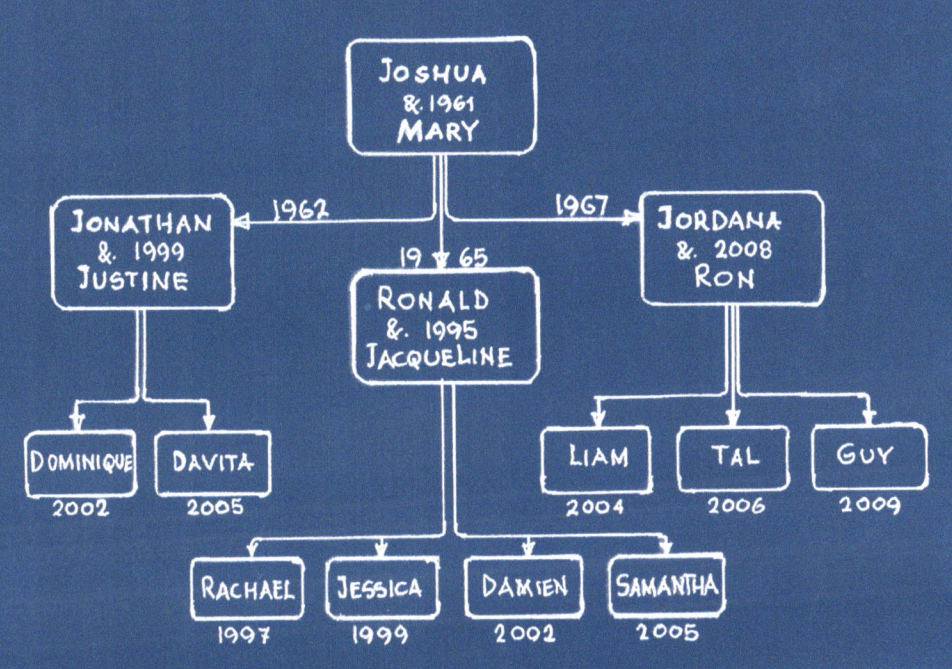

THE PILA FAMILY TREE

*THE GRAVESTONE OF RACHEL, CLEANED BY HER FAMILY
MORE THAN 70 YEARS AFTER HER BURIAL*

AFTERWORD

In July 2016, I travelled with my parents, Mary and Josh, to Poland. We were joined by my daughter, Rachael, my brother, Jonathan (who travelled from England), my sister, Jordana, and my nephew, Liam (who both travelled from Denmark). It was a family pilgrimage of sorts.

I had learnt, heard and spoken about the Holocaust all my life. I had read many books and seen hundreds of films about this bleakest of periods in history. I knew the numbers, the statistics, how many Polish Jews were murdered and how many survived. I was familiar with Auschwitz and the other extermination camps, the gas chambers, and the ovens.

But to know about these things is not the same as seeing them. A picture can tell more than a thousand words when it shines new light on a subject, opening fresh perspectives and avenues of comprehension.

On our trip, we visited many towns and toured the remains of old synagogues and neglected, overgrown Jewish cemeteries. Everywhere we went, the story was the same. Here had been a thriving Jewish community, which had been systematically persecuted and destroyed, its members deported to the death camps. Towns that had been between 30 and 70 percent Jewish were now completely devoid of Jews. A rich and diverse civilisation had come to a sudden and emphatic end.

Towards the end of our tour, we visited the Jewish cemetery in Katowitz, where Josh's sister, my aunt, Rachel, is buried. The cemetery is in a state of neglect and decay. Following directions from the local Jewish Community Centre, we walked through to the far back corner. We had with us a small photo of Josh and Bronia taken at the gravesite in 1946. We used this to identify nearby distinctive tombstones, and to pinpoint the location of Rachel's grave.

Rachel's tombstone was no longer standing, it lay on the ground covered by long grass. No-one had visited her grave for 70 years, there was no-one left to look after it. Experiencing a wide range of emotions, from exhilaration to grief, we pulled away the grass and cleaned the tombstone as best we could.

As we stood by the gravesite, we said *Kaddish*, the traditional mourners' prayer, and were overwhelmed with sadness. We had spent so much time witnessing the evidence of Jewish martyrdom and destruction and visiting cemeteries around the country, and now we were visiting the final resting place of one of our own. This was our cemetery, here lay our martyr.

The Holocaust is almost incomprehensibly immense in scale, but this was our little corner, a focal point for our thoughts and feelings. The waves of emotion that had washed over us throughout our tour finally broke and we all cried. We cried for Rachel and in doing so we cried for every victim of the Holocaust, for our people.

※ ※ ※

*JOSH AND HIS GRANDDAUGHTER RACHAEL
AT HIS SISTER'S GRAVE*

[ABOVE LEFT] MEMORIAL PLAQUE AT THE SOCCER FIELD, SITE OF THE PUNKT
[ABOVE RIGHT] JOSH'S GRANDCHILDREN RACHAEL & LIAM AT HIS SISTER RACHEL'S GRAVESITE
[BELOW] JOSH OUTSIDE BRONIA'S FAMILY APARTMENT ON DEKERTA STREET

The next day, we went on a trip back in time, tracing our Polish heritage. To me it felt like a lightning tour of the Holocaust—the Holocaust in a day.

Sosnowiec

We started the day in Sosnowiec, at the football stadium, the site of the *punkt*. A busload of Israeli and American Jews, members of the Zaglebie World Organization, was visiting the football stadium to hold a short ceremony in honour of their ancestors. We did not know them but we formed an immediate bond, joined by a collective memory of a dark moment in history.

Enthusiastically, we exchanged stories of the places we had visited and our families' histories. Together we sang the *HaTikvah*, the Israeli national anthem, and lit memorial candles. Josh was called to the microphone and asked to address the crowd. All were moved that he was able to give a first-hand account of the events of 12 August 1942.

In Sosnowiec today there are no Jews. Only occasional visitors, discovering their tragic past.

Wolbrom

Next, we travelled to Wolbrom, a small agricultural town 60 kilometres north-east from Sosnowiec. Wolbrom was the birthplace of Solomon's mother, Tova Jacobovich, and two of Solomon's brothers, Usher and Victor. In 1939 there were 4,500 Jews in Wolbrom, comprising 50 percent of the town's population.

In early September 1942, the Jews were forced to gather in the central square for a selection. About 800 Jews were marched into the forest and shot dead in large ditches. The remainder were ultimately deported to Treblinka to die in the gas chambers.

The old synagogue, built in the 1600s, remains intact. As was often the case, the Nazis refrained from destroying the building and instead found a purpose for it, using it as a storehouse. Today, it is a warehouse for a company selling agricultural chemicals. With its fading yellow paint and rundown exterior, the only indication of the building's former glory is the distinctive shape of its windows.

We visited the small Jewish cemetery. Like so many Jewish cemeteries throughout Poland, it had been destroyed by the Nazis, whose aim was not just to wipe out the Jewish community but to also erase all evidence of its past. In recent years, a fence has been erected around the cemetery and some fragments of headstones have been collected and resurrected. A monument to the Holocaust victims of Wolbrom was erected in 1988.

We walked into the forest, following in the footsteps of the condemned. We stood before a large monument to those that had been shot there, the eerie silence of the forest belying the terrifying final moments of the victims.

In Wolbrom today there are no Jews. Hundreds of years of Jewish life have been washed away, with only a few grim reminders, left by survivors who do not want to return but who also do not want to forget.

Wodzislaw

Our next stop was Wodzislaw, a medieval town on the trading route between Krakow and Warsaw, and the home of the Pila family. Solomon was born in Wodzislaw.

The recorded Jewish history of Wodzislaw dates to the 1500s, and the great synagogue on Aryan Street, close to the centre of town, was built in the early 1600s. It would have been a grand and imposing building in its prime, the pride of the local community. Today, a simple sign identifies the ruins as the old synagogue but warns people to keep out because the structure is at risk of collapsing at any moment.

The old Jewish cemetery lay on a hill outside of the town. All the headstones have been removed and a highway now runs through the middle of it. In more recent times, the area of the cemetery on one side of the highway has been fenced off and a monument to the Jewish victims erected.

In 1939, the Jewish population numbered around 3700, approximately 70 percent of the town's population. In late September 1942, a *punkt* was held at the football stadium and the selected Jews were transported to Treblinka.

In Wodzislaw today there are no Jews. All that remains are the ruins of a once-thriving community.

Wislica

Our final stop was Wislica, an ancient town north-east of Krakow. Jews had lived there from the 1500s. Local records of the Lancmans, Bronia's family, date back to the 1750s.

In 1939, 1500 Jews lived in Wislica, approximately 60 percent of the town's population. On 3 October 1942, the Jewish community was liquidated and its members sent to Treblinka.

We walked through an overgrown patch of grass that had been the Jewish cemetery. The gravestones had been removed and used to build roads. Only one remained, a very thick stone that may have been too much trouble to move. The original engraving on the stone had been deliberately scraped off.

Nothing remains of the old synagogue. Where it once stood is now an ugly communist-era block of apartments. In the town's central square is a small monument to the victims of the Nazis. It makes no mention of Jews.

At one end of the square is a church, built in the 1300s. It is a magnificent, imposing building, standing in stark contrast to the modest housing surrounding it. On a wall of a building adjacent to the church we could see that someone had drawn a Star of David, the universal Jewish symbol, hanging from a hangman's scaffold.

In Wislica today there are no Jews. There is nothing to show that Jews ever lived in the town. There is only anti-Semitism. Anti-Semitism without Jews!

***

I was very glad to have visited Poland but not sorry to leave. The country is part of my heritage, but it is not my home. The Polish people welcomed me, but I do not belong. I had no desire to remain on that land soaked in Jewish blood.

Almost every town bears the scars of the country's terrible past. Tortured ghosts roam the countryside, telling their stories to anyone who stops to listen. There are too many stories, the weight of their tragedy is overwhelming. Like the bottom of the ocean, the Jewish history of this land is dark and foreboding, full of memories and loss, too deep to be illuminated by the sun.

RON PILA, 2020

ACKNOWLEDGEMENTS

Writing this book has been an entirely new and rewarding experience for me. It has been an incredibly enjoyable project, not least because of all of the time I have spent with Josh, my father, discussing and exploring his story and the historical context in which events took place. We have spent countless hours together, in truth often venturing widely off topic to discuss politics, philosophy, current affairs and even the share market. We have always been close, but this venture has brought us even closer. I have cherished this time together.

As much as I have enjoyed the process, I don't think I could have completed this project without the help of some very special people. Josh has been unendingly patient in discussing issues, even when I kept revisiting them to gain that extra level of insight. He is also widely read and has a deep knowledge of the relevant historical events, so has often been my first port of call for research. His memory is phenomenal. Time and again, we have come across external references that corroborate his recollections of events that occurred over 75 years ago.

Similarly, my mother Mary has been a tremendous resource in recounting her story and in providing further insight into Josh, Bronia and others.

My wife, Jackie, has offered invaluable support and has helped to keep me task-focused. She has been readily available to review drafts and bounce around ideas. I have most appreciated her input into the human elements of the story. She has a far superior understanding of human nature and emotions than I (she has a background in social work and I am a commercial lawyer—need I say more!).

I have also had excellent input and assistance from Georgie Raik-Allen and Romy Moshinsky of Real Film & Publishing. While I could get my head around writing a narrative, I was unsure how this could be turned into a book. Fortunately, they do know, and their guidance and professionalism has been indispensable in turning my words into a beautiful legacy for future generations.

Finally, I would like to thank my wider group of family and friends for their interest throughout. So many of you have sat stoically while I recounted at length parts of the story or talked about the project. I have been greeted with nothing but enthusiasm and encouragement. For all that patience, I owe you a book. Here it is!

JOSH WITH HIS GRANDCHILDREN

ABOUT THE AUTHOR

Ron Pila is a Melbourne-based lawyer, holding a Bachelor of Science (Computer Science) and a Bachelor of Law (Hons) from the University of Melbourne. Ron spent most of his legal career specialising in technology contracts at one of Australia's leading law firms, Minter Ellison.

Since leaving Minter Ellison in 2014, Ron has had more time to indulge his interests in history and geopolitics. He has also become one of the world's leading experts on the protagonist of this book, his father Josh Pila. While he has extensive experience in reading books, he had absolutely no experience in writing them.

Ron has been married to his wife Jackie for many happy years and they have four gorgeous children, Rachael, Jessica, Damien and Samantha.